OSCAR BONGA NOMVETE

BECOME
an
UNCOMMON
PURPOSE DRIVEN
ACHIEVER

7 KEY STEPS TO BECOME
A PERSON OF EXCELLENCE

Order this book online at www.trafford.com
or email orders@trafford.com

Most Trafford titles are also available at major online book retailers.

First published in the United Kingdom 2009 under the title - Rising to Excellence

www.thejourneyofexcellence.com

Printed in the United States of America.

ISBN: 978-1-4269-6620-0 (sc)
ISBN: 978-1-4269-6621-7 (e)

Trafford rev. 06/20/2011

 www.trafford.com

North America & international
toll-free: 1 888 232 4444 (USA & Canada)
phone: 250 383 6864 ♦ fax: 812 355 4082

DEDICATION

This book is dedicated to my late grandmother Patience Nomvete, who brought me up, believed in me, spoke words of life and hope to me from a young age. Her prayers, her words and her love have kept me strong. *Lala ngoxolo Mkhonde!*

TABLE OF CONTENTS

PREFACE

Someone said to me;

    "I wouldn't bother myself living life being controlled by '*a purpose*' or any rules for that matter, I just let the wind blow, why not chill, take it easy and let life."

I responded;

    "There is nothing wrong with letting the wind blow, the only problem is that the wind blows where it likes. If you are smart, you will prepare your sails and aim them so that it blows you towards the direction you wish to go. At least have a destination in mind, and then let the wind blow. If you don't aim your Sails, the wind will take you anywhere".

I was really being sincere with this guy, I honestly believe that if you begin to pursue a significant goal, you may not become the most famous person in the world but you will certainly become the best you can be with what God has given you. But if you aim at nothing, you will get just that, - Nothing.

If you are going to live life anyway, why not live a life with meaning, passion, significance, adventure, excitement and leave no room for regrets.

Having read a handful of books on many life related issues, I noticed they all spell out that our lives are meant to have a purpose, a reason to live for. That sounds nice, but for many people somehow when it comes to day to day realities, this purpose thing is just artificial, unreal and unattainable. It seems as if only a few very smart individuals were meant to shine. The rest were destined to bum around in their meaningless lives and be tossed back and forth by life as it likes. Well, if this is the case, then our duty boils down to how well we respond to the day to day events of life and how well we interact with people we meet daily while busy in our action, - there lies the value of our story.

Let me invite you to reason with me through the pages of this book;

⊙ Is there something we can do to turn daily events into a meaningful exciting life?

⊙ Could we possibly stretch ourselves to achieve a significant purpose and perhaps grow bigger in the process?

⊙ What if our pursuit for significance is the very secret to enjoying a happy life?

⊙ What exactly can be a suitable purpose to live for, since there is so much one can do during a lifetime?

Well, there are so many different views on how one can discover a suitable purpose to live for. Some people believe that you should pray to God to reveal your purpose.

Others believe that purpose is a matter of upbringing, culture and being programmed by social environment; that determines what you become later as an adult.

While others believe it is all pointless because only a chosen few were predestined to do something meaningful anyway.

Whatever your beliefs are, let us just agree on one thing that from the day you were born to the day you die you will travel through events that will change your life and shape your destiny. Whether you have planned these events or not, they will all together be the purpose you will live your life for. This series of events is called **destiny**. So the question really is;

> Is there anything you can do to maximise your effectiveness given the events that follow from now on?

Why wait for life to take its course instead of being proactive and start your engines and take control of your own life? You can begin today regardless of your age, education or the condition of your bank account. You have no idea what you can become.

Your destiny is not what you will achieve, but what you will become.

This book is simple, easy to read, enjoyable and practical. It will help you discover your purpose, maximise your potential and help you become effective in your field of calling.

My aim for writing this book is to assist you break your own limits and become the best you can be. I trust you will enjoy these principles and the inspiring stories, and use them as a guide in your Journey of Purpose.

-OSCAR BONGA NOMVETE-

INTRODUCTION

THE MAGIC OF A GENIUS

Do you remember those early days of life? Those days if you can still remember, you used to scream awfully, lying on your back without a care in the world. To you the world was yourself, screaming was your invention. You screamed to get all your needs met. It worked effectively every time. Strangely enough, you didn't even know what was so effective about it, for all you cared, it was working.

It had an effect that made your world move to your rhythm. It had such an impact that everyone came to a standstill and gave you all attention you wanted whenever you screamed.

You screamed to get food, attention, love, care and every other thing you wished for. It met all your desires and wants. It was magic. Come to think of it, you had no idea how you even stumbled into using it the first time, but that didn't matter, all that mattered; it was working effectively.

Few months later you had learnt to crawl on the floor, move around and had familiarised yourself with the corners of your world. One day you screamed but ALAS! To your great surprise, this time your scream had no effect, or rather not what you expected. This time your mother looks at you with an annoyed look in her eyes, she shouts back at you, commanding. Though you were not sure what she is saying but you knew whatever she is saying means – NO SCREAMING!

You wondered;
    "What's wrong with her?"
Suddenly you became concerned to get things working for you again. You wanted food, attention, love and care, you wanted it all, and you wanted it now! For some reason your scream was either not loud enough or there was something wrong with your mother's hearing.

So you decided to look into new strategies to get her attention. You added something visual to your screaming. This time you screamed, threw yourself on the floor, rolled around on the floor and guess what? She turned around and looked, picked you off the floor, put you on her chest, with a defeated smile on her face she asked;
    "What's the matter honey?"
Then she gave you food, attention, love and care.

    "Hmm Impressive!" You thought.
    "I have just invented a whole new system to get everything working again, my world is back to just the way I like it. For sure I am a Genius!"

MEET THE GENIUS

After taking a few months thinking hard what to say to your mother, one day you craftily made your first speech;
    "Daaada."

You almost got a standing ovation, for successfully addressing your parents in spite being chauvinistic.

By the time you started nursery, you had changed your success system a few times, because you realised nothing works rigidly for all occasions. And that life demands some **flexibility** and **adaptation**. You knew your strategy well. It worked effectively for every goal, but your mother kept shifting the goal posts. What annoyed you though is that she was changing expectations and goals without even consulting you. However you were just as determined to win in this game called life. You were determined to do whatever it takes to improve your strategy and try as many new ways as it takes to get what you want.

You knew you had to be on top of things and make your needs known otherwise you may be ignored. Well, who knows?

So you became an expert in refining the process of getting things you want, the way you like them. You were so good at it, you knew beyond doubt that you are a Genius!

Early during your primary school days you refined a technique called 'lying' which seemed to outstand all other techniques you had tried before. You had not done your home work, then your nursery teacher asked about it. Bravely, you replied;
"The puppy ate my home work".
She tilted her head looking at you pitifully and said;
"Aahh, I'm so sorry. Oh well, you go then sit next to your friend and look at her homework. We'll have to do something about that dog."

You were delighted at how well this worked. You were impressed at how much success comes just by introducing few new ideas. You were really the master of your world.

All was well, until of course one day your mother discovered 'the secret of your success' and she yelled;
> "Don't you ever lie to me again, lying is bad, and no child of mine is going to be a liar!"

Then you thought;
> "There she goes again, ruining my life, she has to spoil everything just when things are going well for me."

Since you didn't know how she knows you are lying, you decided to cut it down. But you were still determined to live and make success of everything you do and get everything you want. You even came up with more sophisticated strategies such as asking something from Dad privately and get it quickly before Mum finds out. What a Genius!

From the day you were born nothing was impossible for you. You could get anything, pursue any goal and accomplish any dream. You were born with a success engine inside of you. You were born with genes for success. You had in you enough creativity to derive systems to get anything you need and achieve anything you want.

You were born with every ability necessary to help you succeed in your world. You were created with enough genius to be above every situation and solve every problem. You had the ability to rule in your world, and be in control of all activities.

You were born a conqueror, victory was written all over you.

How do I know this?

Because you were made by God. He made all things perfect and made you complete with full potential to triumph, dominate and succeed. Unless of course you don't believe He made you, then I suppose you existed through 'evolution' and therefore are an offspring of Apes. In that case I assume an exception; you have a different kind of potential.

GENIUS LOST IN THE CROWD

As your world got bigger, you had to deal with more people than just Mum and Dad. Your siblings came along to compete for attention. There was school with all its demands. Those red-lipped mistresses who knew everything and ever so ready to dump it all on you. You knew there was something wrong with them insisting on doing home work every day; just that your mother didn't agree with you. Thank God for friends and their wisdom, they understood the true meaning of life;

To play, eat and have fun, and play, eat and have fun.

Your world added all kinds of interesting people, some smart, some intelligent and some just going along as though forced to live. Some got along well with you but others just didn't get your *mojo* and style, and where things went wrong, you weren't bothered, it was never your fault anyway, it was their problem.

You knew deep inside that you are a Genius and you could have anything you want except that now there were more genius tricks required to stay on top of the game. It was getting a bit hard to consistently get what you want. There were too many Success Strategies needed, and too many new ideas required to stay in control.

Life was getting too busy, scattered by all the exciting choices. If you could, you would try out everything, but unfortunately you couldn't, and of course there were always the forbidden trees of life.

THE BATTLE OF THE GENIUS

To succeed in a world of plenty choices meant that you had to use more sophisticated tactics to continue having what you want. The world out there wasn't as easy as twisting Mum and Dad's arm.

Pressure to give in was growing like weed. Not that you were too concerned, as long as you had friends on your side everything was ok. Your new philosophy was;
"If I can't beat them, I might as well join them."

As a teenager, you unconsciously gave in to the habits and addictions of your friends;
It was a small price to pay for acceptance.

By then you had lost control of your own world completely. You started appreciating your friend's lifestyles. They looked 'cool' as if they had it all together. You started learning from friends how to behave, you copied them so much that you become just like them. As a result, your whole environment and friends defined the new you. You were no longer the unique genius who is on top of his or her world. You had become a diluted imitating copycat, but that didn't bother you much. All that mattered was being accepted by friends. You dressed like them, spoke like them and did everything with one purpose in mind;
To please your friends.

Though you were enjoying the company of friends, there were also growing fears inside. You felt secure being accepted by friends but it conflicted with the desire to be different and unique. It conflicted with the desire to do something significant in life that has your name on it. Fears and questions about who you really are popped up now and then. You wondered if you had what it takes to stay accepted by friends. The world around you looked overwhelmingly large, causing doubt if you can ever make it on your own. Life was just happening fast like a rollercoaster. You wondered about your role in life, whether you really needed to be here after all, or if the world could continue without you.

You wondered whether you will ever make a difference in such a fast moving big world. You desired to find meaning in everything and purpose to live for. You desired to do something that can make you shine and set you apart from other people. Something that can distinguish you from the rest, make you happy, rich and famous.

You will find this book exciting and helpful in guiding you fulfil a happy, significant and blessed life. But there is a condition;
> You have to start making the necessary changes in your life immediately.

The book gives Seven Steps to become a Person of Excellence;
❶ Step Out from the Crowd
❷ Recognize the Greater Purposes of God
❸ Rediscover Yourself
❹ Discover and nurture your Personal Genius
❺ Develop an Uncommon Purpose Driven Attitude
❻ Align Yourself with Purpose Centred Success
❼ Recognize and Pursue your Purpose

These Seven Steps are not mutually exclusive. They are workable together without conflict. The Steps are given as signposts to help you mark the milestones of your progress in your own Journey.

If this book finds you still confused about your purpose in life, no need to worry, just get ready to apply the principles discussed and you will soon be on the path to a great future.

Let me encourage you to decide NOW to **pursue your purpose** and **maximise your potential**. Do it;
- For the sake of your family.
- For the sake of your loved ones.
- For the sake of future generations.
- More importantly do it for what you will become as you pursue your purpose.

Well, at this point let us do a quick test; Please stop reading before going to the next paragraph, take a moment and pray;

> Ask God to help you use what you are about to learn to change your life and ask him to help you live to the fullness of your potential. NOW STOP AND PRAY!

I wonder if you really prayed that prayer. If you did not, it is well likely that you will not be using the recommendations that you are about to read. In that case, you may as well close the book and give it to someone who is hungry for change. If you have prayed that prayer, well done! Now you are ready to start the Journey.

PART ONE // SEVEN KEY STEPS TO BECOME A PERSON OF EXCELLENCE

CHAPTER ONE // STEP OUT FROM THE CROWD

THE JOURNEY HAS BEGUN

The Journey of Purpose can get so mixed up and confusing with many detours and unclear direction. Don't get misled when you see people struggling, living hard, busy trying to make it and going nowhere and think;
> "Oh well I'm no different."

It is easy to accept defeat as if you too are trying hard but going nowhere. That is a lie.

The thought of having other people to identify with can become a comforting excuse and make you think;
> "I am just one of them anyway. There is nothing special about me. After all what's the big deal about life, just to live each day and accept whatever life brings along and be happy."

It is that easy to settle for mediocrity.

Let us kill that demon excuse right here right now;
>You are extremely valuable. You are here for a purpose, assigned with a profound mission that cannot be attempted by anyone else but you. You will not fail, you will become all that you were created to become.

A life that is defended by excuses has become comfortable in defeat, it has settled for mediocrity and is destined for failure.

RECOGNIZE MEDIOCRITY

It is not enough to know that Life is a Journey, the key is accepting that you are responsible for the direction of your own journey. You are the driver.

There is no comfort in settling for mediocrity just because you meet a lot of people who look comfortable in their failure. That is complete deception.

If you have considered settling where you are, let this be your turning point. Today is the day you start your journey to a better life, even more importantly - **a journey to becoming the best you can be.**

It's a fact; the easiest thing to do is to go with the flow, just following the majority and friends. It takes **no** hard work to be a people pleaser. But to be different from the crowd is a sign of maturity.

It is comfortable to hide in the crowd, that way you don't have to take responsibility for your decisions. It's a comforting feeling to know you don't have to face the consequences of your own decisions and actions. After all, the Crowd is always welcoming. They call;
>"Come on everybody, join our party train!"

Many people easily jump on to ride the crowd's train without asking questions. This is the kind of people who don't bother to think about tomorrow, they are only concerned about fitting in. They don't think beyond eat, drink, laugh, sleep, get up, get along, and repeat the routine.

A Genius mind is always seeking ways to beat the Crowd. The Genius knows that getting out of the crowd needs;

❶ A tactic to deal with the crowd

❷ A tough and decisive mind, and

❸ Readiness to face new challenges.

It doesn't matter how long it takes or what price it costs, the Genius will make a way because she or he knows that there is no prize for siding with the crowd.

No doubt you don't belong to the crowd, you have proved yourself; here you are reading this book to help you stay free of Crowd's thinking. The Crowd may have their purpose, but it is definitely not yours. You are prepared to live a purposeful life and maximise your potential.

When the Crowd invites you;

"Hey you, come on join in, it's a free ride!"

You ask;

"Where are you all going?"

They say;

"We don't know, but we're sure having fun here?"

You simply move on because you know there is more to life than just eating, drinking and having fun.

MIND THE SPELL OF THE CROWD

The crowd is happy to sit on their potential and dreams and suffer them to die. Now when you decide to pursue your dreams, you are deciding against the interests of the crowd, so you will definitely invite criticism and rejection.

Stepping out must go with **courage**, with a **single minded focus** and a **determined belief** that - **you will certainly make it.**

Dare to step out and give it everything you've got just for the sake of those who will benefit when you have completed the challenge. Be motivated by their smiles because you decided to step out. Just imagine a moment of celebration in the future being surrounded by happy faces because you dared to step out and fulfilled your dream.
What a joy!
That will be your greatest moment!

Mind the Dream Killers

The crowd on the other hand will be casting spells of fear telling you;

> "If you dare leave us you will be lonely out there, you will have no one to support you."

They will bring up all sorts of reasons why you shouldn't follow your dream. They will even ridicule your efforts;

> "You are trying to be something you are not. Who do you think you are? With your kind of background you can't go

too far. You will never amount to anything. You are just wasting your time." They will say.

The crowd can subject you to all sorts of blackmail and fear just to get you to give up your dreams. They can even inflict you with remorse and say;

"Are you trying to reject us now heh? Are you trying to show us you are better than us? Well then, when you fail, don't forget we warned you. Good luck dreamer."

The experience of dealing with the crowd can be isolating and draining. Sometimes even your own family can act part of the crowd. When you share your intentions to pursue a big dream with your family, they may give you lukewarm response and water down your dream. In Genesis Chapter 37, Joseph had this experience when he shared his dream with his family. His own brothers plotted to murder him saying;

"Let's kill this dreamer, who does he think he is?"

To them, he was better dead than fulfilling a greater purpose. They ultimately sold the future Prime Minister of Egypt for 20 pieces of silver into slavery trying to stop him from stepping into his destiny. But for Joseph being sold into slavery or even being in jail was not going to stop him. He was completely sold out to his dream.

Sometimes the Crowd stops you because they don't understand that you stepping into your destiny is also for their benefit. If Joseph had not been tenacious in pursuing his dream, his mother and father and all his brothers together with their children would have been wiped out by drought and poverty. This would mean there would be no nation of Israel today, but Joseph was resilient, he would not give into his brothers' discouraging spells. He decided to fulfil his purpose whatever the cost, and therefore saved a generation. You too can dare to step out.

The Crowd only wonders about with no definite plans for the future but the Genius takes the time to think about how he or she can make a difference.

Challenge yourself to the risk of being alone in your destiny. Be brave. Step out in faith. Step out in courage. Step into action. Step into larger life. **The greatest tragedy is not that you will fail, it is failing to step out and get started, because you will never know what you could have become.**

It must be painful when you have to wave goodbye to your own family because they are playing crowd, but but what good is it for you to keep company with people who want to subject you to mediocrity?

You alone are responsible for your own future.

At the same time it is not easy for parents to get excited when their child says something like;
> "I am going to be a Prime Minister."

A typical parent response is;
> "Shut up and eat your vegetables, go to school and stop day dreaming."

They water down such dreams really to protect their baby from disappointments of life. Probably because they are using themselves as a point of reference. They had dreams but failed to step out to fulfil them. They got discouraged by the crowd and gave in, or they faced challenges somewhere along the way and gave up. Joseph suffered rejection from his family because his dream exceeded family expectations. No one in his family was expected to grow into leadership to rule even over Mum and Dad. It just sounded like an insult for him to dream that even his parents will be subject to his leadership, so his brothers took it upon themselves to kill that silly dream together with the dreamer.

THE GREATEST TRAGEDY IS NOT THAT YOU WILL FAIL, IT IS FAILING TO STEP OUT AND GET STARTED, BECAUSE YOU WILL NEVER KNOW WHAT YOU COULD HAVE BECOME.

Decision Time

It may be that your decision to step out does not come without a cost. Friends may reject you. Friends don't clap hands when one friend steps into change even if the change is for better, they fear losing a good friend. So to try and fix the situation, they stop the friend from changing. You may find yourself at a point where you have to decide whether to drag your friends along with you or kiss them goodbye. The sooner you give up your friendship with Dream Killers, the better for you.

It can be pretty heavy to invite a crowd into a journey that you yourself have not yet travelled; Much like Moses experience with the Israelites when they demanded to go back to Egypt halfway to the Promised Land. They opposed him, fought him, argued, and delayed him so much that he ended up not making it to his destination, - the promised land.

9

Never conform to the thinking of the crowd, never give in to their demands, and never accommodate their mediocrity.

MAJORITY IS NOT ALWAYS RIGHT

The 'majority effect' gives an impression that since everyone seems to believe in a particular idea, then it must be right. Common people assume whatever friends decide on is probably good for them too. But, the opposite is what makes Uncommon People superior;

⊙ Their ability to reject the mind of the crowd.

⊙ Their ability to decide independently.

⊙ Their willingness to pay any price for their dreams.

This minority three percent of the world's population and elite people have long decided to reject the comfort of the crowd and mediocrity. They know that **tolerating mediocrity is as dangerous as inviting failure.** They continuously look for meaningful ways to make their lives count;

⊙ They examine the purpose behind every activity.

⊙ They are Go-getters.

⊙ They are Goal Setters and goal oriented.

⊙ They live in pursuit for higher purpose, in pursuit of excellence, prosperity and uncommon life.

TOLERATING MEDIOCRITY IS AS DANGEROUS AS INVITING FAILURE.

Uncommon Achievers know that a life that tolerates mediocrity can never improve. They don't get persuaded by the crowd, they refuse to think with the mind of the crowd. This is the club in which you belong, because by reading this book you have made a choice to reject the influence of the crowd and start your journey towards personal excellence.

CHAPTER TWO // RECOGNISE THE GREATER PURPOSES OF GOD

THERE IS A PURPOSE FOR EVERYTHING GOD CREATED

Have you ever noticed that your dog pet 'Skippy' does not struggle being a dog or try hard to fulfil its dog purpose. Skippy is naturally friendly to the owner, barks at strangers and does not have to go to dog school to train on what to do, its all 'natural instincts'. With exception to special dog skills such as leading a blind person and police work, otherwise dogs are born with 'purpose instincts'.

Your cat does not have many worries when getting up in the morning other than to mew, eat its food and out hunting for mice. It comes naturally.

If you enjoy cartoons like me, you will be familiar with Tom and Jerry. Tom the cat is forever chasing after the little mouse Jerry. The chase gets so fierce leaving your heart pounding fearing for little Jerry's life, thinking if Tom catches that poor Jerry it's all over, he will have him on his plate for dinner. The chase goes on and on, but at the climax when the moment comes for Tom to kill his prey; the two ironically always end up negotiating a settlement where Jerry walks free. In this cartoon Tom and Jerry break the natural mouse and cat rules. It is absurd for a cat to negotiate with a mouse. After all the hard chasing Tom and Jerry end up lying on each other's laps cuddling. After all your heart pounding, sweating, dreading to witness a mouse being murdered, you end up saying;

"aaahh isn't that sweet".

You worry that if Tom ever catches that little Jerry the fun is over. But, of course it never happens.

In real life every cat is driven by an instinct to catch and kill the mouse. The cat knows it and the mouse knows it too. Every dog has an instinct to befriend the owner and bark at suspicious strangers. They know it from birth. It is true for every other animal. A cow produces milk and gives it freely without asking;

"But why me?"

And so every other animal has an inborn instinct which defines its purpose in life. **But human purpose is not defined by instincts, it is assigned by God and discovered by you.**

DOES GOD REALLY CARE IF YOU LIVE A PURPOSE CENTERED LIFE?

The answer is a resounding YES!

It is a concern to God when the people He created and gave life are struggling to find meaning to life. **Everything God has made has a purpose; nothing He has made is without a purpose.** He is a purpose driven God in all He does. It is a concern to God when people who are made in his image, bearing his brand name are not

reflecting his purposefulness, his excellence, his streak of victory and winning spirit. It is heart breaking to God when people are losers, strugglers and victims of the same life he has given to them.
"But the people who know their God shall prove themselves strong and shall stand firm and do exploits" (Daniel chapter 11 verse 31; Amplified Bible).

It is **not** God's plan for people to be confused about the future or be uncertain about their lives.

His plan is that people may prosper and his gift to humanity is life and hope for a bright future (Jeremiah 29:11). He has supplied everything necessary for you to succeed, to prosper, and to be victorious. He has made available to you every good principle to help you prosper and find your way out of the mess into a purposeful destiny.

EVERYTHING GOD HAS MADE HAS A PURPOSE; NOTHING HE HAS MADE IS WITHOUT A PURPOSE.

Deuteronomy chapter 30 verse 19 says;
"...I have placed before you both life and death *but choose life.*"

God's name is only glorified when people are successful and prospering than when people are struggling, living purposelessly trying to make it day after day. He has provided means of escape from confusion, poverty, uncertainty, pain, anguish and frustrations and all you have to do is decide to get out of the mess. His true desire is to see you live purposefully, victoriously and prosperously.

God really wants you to prosper, not just for prosperity's sake or selfish reasons but so that you can become a blessing to others and thus displaying his glory.

God's Plan for you

There is a definite purpose for your existence, when you are busy fulfilling it you will find fulfilment and happiness. God wants you to succeed, but He would not want you to succeed just for the sake of success, it is important that you succeed within purpose. It is God's primary interest is to see you out of the crowd, clutter and confusion, into a life that boldly stands out to reflect His glory. The ball now is in your court, it is you who should make the move. Make a decision to live a life that is purpose driven and start to use your God given potential to fulfil a significant purpose.

But now be careful that you don't start a wild-goose chase on searching for purpose, making it a complicated dilemma like decoding a bedlam. You don't need sleepless nights trying to figure out why you were born. Simply get ready to respond to what comes naturally as we explore issues of purpose and excellence.

IT IS GOD'S PRIMARY INTEREST TO SEE YOU OUT OF THE CROWD, CLUTTER AND CONFUSION, INTO A LIFE THAT BOLDLY STANDS OUT TO REFLECT HIS GLORY.

In the 12th verse of Jeremiah 29 there is a promise that can change your life;

> "If you seek me with all your heart, I will be found by you".

Why would you want to find God?

For many reasons really; many history-makers and world changers sought God thoroughly and found solutions to some of the world's problems, and also found direction for their lives. As for you right now, you need him to guide you towards your purpose in life. He is happy to reveal it to you. It is on top of his agenda that you find your purpose in life. He wants only the best for you. The fact that you are now reading this book is one of his means to help you step into your purpose. Now the only thing standing between you and God's best for your life, is yourself.

Start today to seek him, and seek him diligently, you will be happy with the outcome.

EXPLORING ISSUES OF IDENTITY, PURPOSE AND FINAL DESTINATION

At age 20, I remember attending a *Youth For Christ* rally in Johannesburg, being challenged by the rally Speaker Sean Daly. He made a very short but powerful speech which changed the way I viewed life from that day.
He said;

> "To succeed at this University of Life, you must resolve three requirements;
> One - *Your Identity*,
> Two - *Your Purpose for living*, and
> Three - *Your Final Destination*.

If you fail to organise and settle these requirements, you will
have missed the very reason for your existence".

As he went to sit down ending his speech within 30 seconds, it
suddenly hit me like a ton of bricks that we actually have only one
life, one chance, just one and the show is over, no rehearsals, no
repeats, no reruns. I sat there thinking;
"I don't know how, but I've got to make my life count."
Right that moment I made my decision to step out of my mediocre
life, out of the comfort of my own crowd and told myself it is time
to take control of my future and destiny.

THE TRUTH ABOUT YOUR IDENTITY

Sean's speech was proposing a settlement of three unforgiving
issues;
- Self identity
- Purpose for living, and
- One's Final Destination.

Why are these three particularly important to us?
Well, let's explore them a little deeper.

Since the objective of this book is to discuss issues relating to
Purpose and Excellence, Sean's second question on purpose will be
addressed in depth later. For now let's look briefly at what Identity
and Destination are about without losing track of our journey.

Self Identity

Self identity in its simplest definition is self knowledge or self
realisation. It answers the question - Who am I?

Going back to our illustration of Cats and Dogs, we said that Skippy doesn't spend effort figuring out what he is, which language to speak whether to bark or to grunt. Dogs just open their mouth and out comes woof! They have no problems with tribal and racial identity. They are born dogs, they are happy as dogs. They speak doggy language, their identity is clear. The only other thing important to them is their name. Once they know their call name, their identity is complete regardless who the father was or what the mother's maiden name was. Whether the father was married to the mother. That is all irrelevant to them and will not affect their confidence or performance in life. God made it so easy and straight forward for animals, they are what they are and they accept it that way, no problems.

God did not make it necessarily hard for human beings instead he gave us something that no dog has; **the power of choice**, the ability to think, the ability to learn, to reason, to decide for ourselves, and choose what is best for us. The power to choose what we want to be and how we want to live our lives. **Human life is all about choices**.

The power of choice comes with two things; **Responsibility** and **Consequences**. For every choice we make we can expect resulting outcomes and therefore we better make responsible choices.

The God Factor inside of you

We also have something greater within us which dogs wish for but can't get, - **the spirit of God**. According to the Bible; He made men in his own image and breathed into men and men became a living being. He did not breathe into any dog. Because of the nature of human beings having the spirit of God in them, spirituality automatically becomes part of what defines human identity. **We are**

spirit beings with a physical nature, and therefore it is impossible to define our identity and exclude the God Factor. Remember dogs are just flesh and bones, with dog breath. They need not get spiritual about life, it won't work. But for human beings not getting spiritual about life just doesn't work instead it makes human beings become like animals. The spirit being in us is hundred percent part of our identity and who we are. It forms the primary definition of Human Identity. Who we are in the family tree, tribal group, race, all come secondary.

For human beings, having unclear identity affects not only their self esteem but also how well one functions in life, in society, in marriage, in career and other spheres of life. This definitely includes how well we function in our purpose in life, if at all we ever begin to function purposefully. This highlights just how important it is to know who you are and to realise your Identity. **Knowing your identity is the starting point to living a fulfilled life.**

WE ARE SPIRIT BEINGS WITH A PHYSICAL NATURE, AND THEREFORE IT IS IMPOSSIBLE TO DEFINE OUR IDENTITY AND EXCLUDE THE GOD FACTOR.

The Final Destination

The third and last issue raised by Sean's speech brings us to the question of life's destination. There are many speculations about 'life after death'. Tons of books and movies have been written about what people imagine is life after death but this book will not be dealing with this subject. Where you go after death has very little to do with purpose and excellence but if you did know, it would affect your attitude towards life.

Our final destination is **not** a matter of chance, some accidental, mysterious, roll a dice, 'only God knows' outcome. It is **not** a decision made by St Peter after scratching his head at the 'Pearly gates' if he exists at all. It is a planned destination decided and organised by you yourself. If life is a journey, then there must be a destination. There are two well known destinations; heaven and hell.

Heaven being the place of God's presence and hell being a place of separation from God.

In John chapter 14 verse 6 Jesus declares himself the only way to heaven;

> "I am the way, the truth and the life. No one can come to the Father except through me."

Further in Romans chapter 10 verse 9 the Bible says if one believes in their heart that Jesus is Lord and acknowledges it by saying;

> "Jesus is Lord"

Then they will be saved.

So this should solve the problem, we no longer need to cross fingers and touch wood hoping that God willing He will let us into heaven. It just settles the record clearly; He is willing and wants us to go to heaven if we are willing. By simply choosing to accept the offer made by Jesus in Romans chapter 10 verse 9 then *voila!* You are on your way to heaven.

Such a simple act also initiates your personal relationship with God, which in turn will influence your productivity in life.

YOUR PURPOSE EXISTED FIRST BEFORE YOU

An inventor invents because she or he is driven by necessity, as the cliché goes - *necessity is the mother of invention*. Necessity determines how the inventor's device is going to be used or how the device will work. Its purpose, function and intended use are all known prior to its invention. So the reason why a particular object should be made is determined by the need for that particular object. **Purpose precedes invention**. No inventor designs an object and then scratch his or her head to figure out how to use it. First they have a purpose in mind, then invention follows. The shape, the design, the length, the weight and every feature about the object is specific to the function and purpose of the object.

In the same logic, God the creator has designed all that exists around us for a specific purpose. Even the invisible creation is created and designed for a particular purpose. Each and every person in the world was brought to this earth for a specific purpose.

You were created because there was a need that called for a solution in the form of you. There is a function that needs a particular creature with your exact features to fit the purpose. This function will remain undone if you decide to bunk out of your designated purpose.

God has designated everything to fit within his bigger plan and purpose for all creation. It is important that every creature takes its position to maintain smooth running of all creation and to maintain God's grand purpose for all things.

> *GOD HAS DESIGNATED EVERYTHING TO FIT WITHIN HIS BIGGER PLAN AND PURPOSE FOR ALL CREATION.*

YOU HAVE AN APPOINTMENT WITH YOUR ASSIGNMENT

Medical statistics indicates that the probability that you would be born is so slim that your being alive today is only a miracle. **It can only be because you really have to be here.** Your being alive today is evidence that you are here for something significant, regardless how you came to be here.

Let me use myself as an example;
I was a child that my father didn't want to have nor associate with. His family disapproved of his courtship to my mother and in fear he called the courtship off, and the two parted ways meantime my mother was already pregnant. As a result of the events I never got to meet him to this day; however I lived because I had a purpose to fulfil with or without my father's involvement.

My grandmother who brought me up tells me, I was born blind with blood red eyes, a premature at seven months, so fragile, so tiny I could hardly fill up the palm of her hand. She would carry me on one hand while giving me a bath, praying that I would live. She feared I wouldn't survive post-birth challenges, but I lived. Come to think of it, it was in those circumstances that she gave me my name - Bonga, meaning give thanks in all things. I had to survive to serve my purpose and serve you with this material.

Apparently, I was the first baby to be allowed to life by my mother, the previous unwanted pregnancies were aborted. Did my mother suddenly have a special affection for this particular foetus? I guess not. I think she had enough reasons to get rid of this one, especially because the father was no longer interested. I believe I was spared for a purpose. But my survival story is not unique; it is insignificant compared to heart moving circumstances that other courageous people have endured to be alive today.

So you may ask this question;
Can a child born unwanted by parents really live a significant life? Since such a child is not likely to have a caring family environment anyway, in some cases such children never even go to school. But, you better believe it;

> **No baby is born without a significant purpose, and just as well nothing happens without a reason.**

Every child has an appointment with destiny. **Your background does not have to be perfect for you to fulfil your destiny.**

Whatever your story, regardless how tragic you were born, regardless what you have gone through to be alive today, you can only appreciate that you are alive because you were spared for a purpose.

THERE IS A PROBLEM THAT NEEDS YOUR GENIUS

You are what the world has been waiting for. You had to be born to bring progress to the world, to serve your generation. You have a right to be here. Your position in the world has your name on it. You had to be born at the time you were born, in the town or village you were born. Think about the Israelites who were in slavery for 400 years in Egypt. Their rescuer Moses could not have been born 200 years of their slavery, nor could he be born 500 years later. He was born exactly at the right time because the prophecy given to Jacob the father of the slaves was specific that his offspring will be in slavery for 400 years.

Isaac Newton the physicist had to be born in his specific time, in that particular generation to help the world discover laws of physics.

Bill Gates could not have been born before computer age; he would be so bored and out of place. His purpose had to do with computers and therefore he was born in the era of technological revolution.

It's Time to Manifest

You are alive at this time because your life's assignment is for this time, for this generation. In the same logic you had to be born from that particular mother and father for you to have the necessary genes required for your assignment in life. Your assignment in life requires that you go through the life experiences you have gone through as your special training and preparation. Now it is your time to manifest. This is your moment to occupy your place in the world, the whole creation is waiting for you to make your appearance.

I get fascinated watching the discovery channel, how wild animals live and survive in the jungle. Just how the creator has set the ecosystem so complete in itself, yet none of the animals has any education. They don't go to Jungle school to learn how to live purposefully yet they do. I marvel at how they meet each other's needs even though they don't exchange cash for their services. Each animal is specifically shaped for its environment and fits its purpose. In my view it all displays the wisdom and mastermindedness of God. The Beaver chops large trees down so that there's enough wood for the squirrels to build their nests. Lions hunt for food so that the Vultures can have dinner for free. Everything just works together.

> *YOU ARE ALIVE AT THIS TIME BECAUSE YOUR LIFE'S ASSIGNMENT IS FOR THIS TIME, FOR THIS GENERATION.*

You too have a role to play which will benefit this generation and the people you are meant to serve. If you are not yet active in your purpose, it will all come together as you embrace the idea that you are the answer the world has been praying for.

YOU ARE THE PERFECT DESIGN CUT FOR YOUR ASSIGNMENT

Your features are all part of the specifications that make you the right person for your assignment. The pitch of your voice, your height, your weight, the curves of your body and the colour of your eyes; The sharpness of your eye sight, the way you smile, the size of your lips, I can go on.

Your built and every detail about you is designed to accomplish your purpose. Your whole appearance including features that come from your race, tribe and earthnicity are all part of the package specific for the purpose you were born for. The shape of your nose is certainly not an error of nature, it is supposed to shape like that for all the breathing you will be doing fulfilling your purpose, regardless if they like it or not. Tough!

You are altogether a complete package delivered to the world to serve this generation. You have already within you everything it takes to accomplish your mission in life. Every resource you will need is already inside of you. You are adequately equipped for your purpose. You have the determination, the tenacity, the patience, the discipline, the articulation, the physical strength and every other necessary requirement is already inside of you. **To unleash the powerful force within you, you need to cultivate your potential to its capacity and you will be surprised what you can accomplish.** Other than that, there will not be another better version of "you" coming in some future generation. If you fail to deliver your best in this life, you have denied the world of knowing what you were about.

TO UNLEASH THE POWERFUL FORCE WITHIN YOU, YOU NEED TO CULTIVATE YOUR POTENTIAL TO ITS CAPACITY AND YOU WILL BE SURPRISED WHAT YOU CAN ACCOMPLISH.

You are not a prototype or a 'demo' version of yourself. You are not some test dummy here to try out life. You are the real thing. The Genius that the world has been waiting for.

It is important that you give nothing less than your best. Do it because you can. **Settling for a mediocre life will cost you not knowing how much you could have done.** You owe it to yourself to appreciate the opportunity to be alive. It is your personal responsibility **not** to neglect your purpose. **It is one of life's biggest sins to neglect your God given potential, so don't commit it.**

Gifts, Abilities and Talents

In Mathew Chapter 25 the bible has a story about a Master Investor who gave three men each a number of talents (currency) to invest.

Two of the men invested their portions and made interest, but one of them kept the original capital untouched and gave it back to the investor as is. The Master Investor was furious at the man who gave back the original capital. The man had decided to protect the investment (capital), he did not invest it in fear that he could lose it. However the Master Investor was very unhappy with his idea and furiously told him, – he was a cruel man, for not even putting his money in the bank to generate some interest. The Master Investor took his investment seed (of one talent) from the cruel man and gave it to the man who had generated the highest returns from his original capital of five talents.

What do you think made the Master Investor so upset with the man who kept his investment seed untouched? I believe the Master Investor meant;

> "You were so negligent with the seed I gave you that you do not deserve to get anything. Because of your negligence even what you have right now must be taken away from you and be given to someone who is responsible enough to use it."

Think about this, it is critical that you do not neglect your potential. Take responsibility over your gifts, talents and skills because they are the seeds that God has planted in you to cultivate and nurture. There within you lies unlimited potential, and seeds to the greatest achievements the world has yet to witness, if you dare to take the risk and use them.

CHAPTER THREE // REDISCOVER YOURSELF

KNOW YOUR IDENTITY

Bicycle riders who ride just for fun accept any bike as good enough if it has two wheels, if it is the right size, has handlebars and can maintain balance. It only has to take them from point 'A' to 'B' and the job is done. However for expert cyclists such as professional racing cyclists, details count significantly. Before they buy a bike they scrutinise the frame, check the weight and the strength of the frame. They scrutinise the wheels to see if they are alloy or steel, and test the strength of the tyres. Every element matters. And the most important check is the brand name check. A brand name carries in it the certification that the designers of each part are approved by the manufacture as credible and reliable, and therefore the bike is reliable. Their objective is to be sure that they know enough about the bike, and gain confidence that it is able to give them victory during the race. No surprises allowed. The goal is to both finish the race and to win.

Your performance in the race of life is influenced by how well you know yourself.

Since you are the key instrument to fulfilling your destiny, it is absolutely necessary that you scrutinize and test your abilities. In the race of life it is important to be confident of who you really are, how strong you are, what you are capable of, your strengths and weaknesses, what temptations you can't resist, and so on. It is all important preparations for the journey. You don't want to let yourself down with unnecessary setbacks that you could have avoided. The journey is long and testing. When you know your own strengths and weaknesses, you are better prepared to handle challenges and setbacks.

Self Analysis

Self discovery is having a better understanding of your overall potential, a better understanding of your Strengths and Weaknesses, Opportunities available to you and any Threats that could potentially destroy your efforts to succeed. This is known as the SWOT analysis.

S- Strengths: Such as Natural Abilities, Skills and Talents.

W- Weaknesses: *Physical Limitations* - (such as a Disabilities, Tallness, Voice weakness and so on).
Mental Limitations - (such as Memory Deficiency, Attention Deficiency Syndromes).

O- Opportunities: *Hereditary Opportunities* - (such as High IQ, Physical Attractiveness)
External Opportunities - (Such as Wealthy Parents, Encouraging Relationships and Inspiring Associations)

T- Threats: *Self-imposed Threats* - (Such as Bad Habit and Addictions)

Environmental Threats – (Such as Poor Family, Unproductive Social Setting, Unmotivated Associations)

The Human Design

Knowing yourself is understanding how you were made, engineered, how you perform under pressure and most importantly; knowing who you are in God's perspective. When you don't know who you are, you can't attempt to become bigger. People who fail to discover their true identity have no chance of living significant lives.

A Human Being is formed of three Components;
- ⊙ Spirit
- ⊙ Body and
- ⊙ Soul.

The Body is the Visible Part of you.
The Soul is Emotions, Mind and Will.
Your Spirit is the God-breathed part of you. Roughly without going into details, that completes the Human System.

The Bible says God made Adam's Body from the dust and breathed into his nostrils a Life giving Spirit and Adam came alive. God made us Human Beings in his own Image. So your true identity can only be measured by your likeness to God. This realisation is enough for you to ignore issues of Race, Colour, Background as defining your true potential.

Your True Potential

Your true potential is defined only by what God says you can do, and you can do all things. However, we always seek to define our identity and potential in relation to our genealogy, family tree, parents' potential rather than that what God says. We prefer to define our strengths based on our culture, nationality, family and race, rather than what God says we are capable of. If we are born of poor parents, we feel unqualified to hold our chin high because our parents amounted to nothing. We reject our true identity which is likeness to God, but we are willing to accept likeness to our parents as a reflection of our true worth. We assume their abilities as ours, and accept their limitations as our limitations. Sadly we've got things all upside down.

YOUR TRUE IDENTITY CAN ONLY BE MEASURED BY YOUR LIKENESS TO GOD.

It would help you to know that the abilities placed within you by God remain untapped, unchanged and irrevocable regardless of those of your parents. According to the Bible, we can do all things whether we accept this truth or not. Once God has given, he does not take back, whether you decide to use your abilities or take them to the grave unused, it is up to you. They are yours to use or to waste.

Doctor Myles Monroe, the author of *Releasing your Potential* says;
        "The richest ground in the world is the graveyard".
Why?
Because many people lying dead in the graveyards never fulfilled their full potential. Many did nothing with their talents, they failed to convert their potential into dreams and all that potential got buried with them.

YOUR PAST CAN BE MESSY BUT YOUR FUTURE IS A CLEAN PAGE

Self realisation is knowing that you are a unique creature assigned to the world with unlimited potential, unique strengths regardless who your parents are, regardless what race you are or what social class you belong, or what your parents have or have not.

You are not a copy, you are completely original. The unique print on your fingers is a sign that you are not a duplicate. You need to appreciate your uniqueness, accept and believe that your life has a unique purpose and existence. Your DNA print has never been duplicated since Adam.

Self realisation is coming to terms with the fact that you have more potential in you than you can use during your lifetime.

You just have to embrace this truth, there is something special about you.

Forget the Past

Your parents were used as a vehicle to deliver you to the world. They played a role in a setup scene to bring you on board, but they have their own potential different from yours, you have your own. You do not have to be like them or behave like them or do as they did. You do not have to pursue their dreams or measure your life in their standards. You can choose to raise the standard or drop it.

Believe in yourself and in your own possibilities. Becoming an Uncommon Achiever is a result of Self Belief. You can never rise beyond the picture you hold about yourself.

The environment and neighbourhood where you grew up do not have to define what you will become. You can choose to be deferent. Someone said;

> "You can take me out the hood, but you cannot take the hood out of me."

Well this may be true to an extent but everyone has a choice to improve on their background and change for a better future. Poverty does not have to be part of your future just because you were born in a poor community. You can choose to be greater than the average expectations of your community.

Once I challenged a young South African after he made some racist remarks then blamed his parents for his attitude saying;

> "I am a racist, this is who I am, I was born like this, brought up like this, I am never going to change."

I replied saying;

"You have a right to change, you have a right to challenge your upbringing. You are not stuck in the opinions of your parents."

People tend to think that they are stuck with the beliefs of their upbringing, or the beliefs of their race, parents or social class. It is your choice to set a new record in your family or neighbourhood, by deciding to take a distinctly new direction.

Aim to reach the pinnacle of your potential. **Your future cannot be limited by your past. The seeds of greatness are inside of you regardless of your past.** You have a right to live a better life, you can write your own history. **You can never successfully advance forward looking backwards.**

YOUR BACKGROUND DOES NOT DETERMINE THE QUALITY OF YOUR FUTURE

In the animated movie Madagascar, some wild animals were in transit from New York zoo to some eastern country when a fateful shipwreck accidentally lands them at the wild Island of Madagascar. The young lion, the zebra, the giraffe and other zoo friends had never been outside of New York. They had no idea how life is like in the jungle. In the New York zoo, every supper time they were assured of a fair portion of juicy steak dished to each without arguments or fights. No hunting skills were required. There was no king of the zoo, everybody was just friends and everyone in equal ranks. No eating one another, in fact it would be a terrible taboo just to desire the flesh of someone else. They had been living in perfect harmony in New York since they were kids, however to their surprise, in the jungle of Madagascar everything was deferent. There were no friendships between Zebras and Lions. In the jungle your looks determine who you should associate with. There are ranks of power between animals, Lions are kings. Food is not delivered on a plate by the jungle warden, everyone must go hunting; a job that was very hard for the urbanised New York friends. What was more horrifying to the sweet lion from New York is that his best friends are seen as delicious dinner by other lions. This is the law of the jungle.

The movie is a hilarious animation but depicts a picture of animals with a limited mindset. They all protested against jungle life but since they were the only few with a different mindset, they decided to change. The New York giraffe fell in love with a lady giraffe and got married. The lion rediscovers himself as king in Madagascar. When they decided to change, they gradually unlearned the zoo life of New York embraced the jungle lifestyle and prospered.

Everyone can improve regardless of limitations placed by their upbringing. The future is a clean page full of new opportunities. The future has many discoveries to be made and new horizons still to be explored. There are new dimensions of joy and exciting possibilities still ahead.

BE FREE OF LIMITATIONS IMPOSED BY THE PAST

The environment where you grew up and your family background played a role in shaping your current thinking. You see the world not as it is, but through the eyes your background and past experiences.

You interpret all that happens around you and what happens to you based on your past experiences. For an example if as a child you grew up in a less approving home, perhaps your parents did not notice when you did something right but noticed when you went wrong. Or if you were often criticised when you gave your opinion or when you attempted to do something new, then as an adult you are more likely to feel insecure, unsure of yourself, showing symptoms of needing other people's approval and attention. Every adult has trails from their past affecting the way they think and behave.

Shake off the Shackles of the Past

For you to be in control of your future you need to identify and shake off the Shackles from your past, and confront feelings of insecurity, inferiority and self doubt. Being in Christ entitles you to a complete makeover, a total healing from inside out. The old disappears and the new you emerges. Just ask him for healing, ask him to deal with your past. His plan for you is to give you hope and future.

To fully realise new possibilities coming ahead, you must take an objective look at why you think the way you do, your attitudes; why you do the things you do, and challenge yourself to new thinking. To have a good perspective of yourself, first get rid of any negative thoughts you hold about yourself. Eliminate all negative images and memories from the past and get rid of people's opinions of you. Abusive childhood memories have a strong influence on one's self worth, but Children who receive warm parental attention grow up to become confident independent adults.

If you suffered rejection and abuse as a child, find a way to get rid of those feelings of rejection and somehow forgive those who abused you otherwise such memories will hold you back from becoming the best you can be.

My colleague Rita was a tall, slim, modelsome girl who got depressed every time she thought about her family. Even though Rita had an eye catching beauty she struggled consistently with self confidence.

She could not remember a single nice word her mother ever said to her, except a nickname 'Sticks' - because she was so tall and slim. Her self confidence had been blurred by her abusive past. All she imagined about herself was an ugly thin tall girl who would struggle to find a suitable man to love her. Rita also suffered some emotional scars from being abused sexually by a family friend as a child. All these experiences traumatised her so much that even though she was now an adult let alone so beautiful, she dislikes herself with a passion. She could not accept anything good about herself; her self esteem was shattered. She deliberately ate excessively to gain weight trying to lose her childhood name 'Sticks', even though the name was no longer used.

The Turning Point

Rita's story is just one of many stories of people who during their childhood were made victims by people who abused them verbally, sexually, physically or some other ways. If you have suffered similar abuse in your past or have suffered abuse of any kind, I strongly advise that you find a good pastor in a local church or a professional counsellor who can help you deal with your childhood experiences, or alternatively speak to a mature friend who can help you deal with these kinds of issues. If such experiences are not dealt with from the root, they definitely have a negative effect on your performance in life. They will confine you to a *'holding pattern'* when you really want to move to a happier and bigger life, so get up and get help.

Paul who fulfilled a great purpose during his lifetime, co-writing many books in the New Testament made this profound statement about his past;

"This one thing I do: I forget what lies behind and reach forward to what lies ahead". (Phil 3:13)

Destiny is not what has already happened, it is what lies ahead.
However it can be hard to focus on what lies ahead when the wounds of the past have not properly healed, somehow every movement you make provokes the unhealed wounds. So deal with the wounds first and get rid of them so you can be free to enjoy a healthier, brighter and prosperous future.

Who can heal better than the one who made the heart, who can understand the depth of your brokenness better than the one who gave you the soul?

"He heals the broken hearted and binds up their wounds." (Psalm Chapter 147 verse 3, New International Version).

DESTINY IS NOT WHAT HAS ALREADY HAPPENED, IT IS WHAT LIES AHEAD.

KNOW YOUR WORTH

Discovering your true identity begins with knowing your creator. If you seek God your creator, your manufacturer, and understand his expertise and abilities, it will help you realise the quality of Product you are, the nature of creature you are. The quality of a Product is determined by the expertise of the Manufacturer.

There are not enough books written to explain the potential and the abilities of God your maker. If you could realise the depth of his supremacy, you would understand your own value and esteem. In Psalms chapter 82 verse 6 the Bible says you are gods, and all of you are sons of the most high.

Think about it, God's power, his potential, His nature and his abilities are in you. We can't even begin to explore all of his abilities; from creating all things we see around us, to creating all the galaxies beyond what the eye can see. How He moulded a human being from the dust, designing the human anatomy, connecting the nervous system together with billions of brain cells to function like they do. Just how He made the elements of your body to communicate to one another even when you sleep. We don't have enough pages in this book to write about His expertise, neither do I have the writing skill to paint the picture that portrays His true potential and magnificence. He is simply Supreme and unlimited in everyway. What matters most is knowing that you were made in His image and likeness, and inherited His abilities. His expert power is in you. You can excel like Him and be as outstanding as he is. Therefore **nothing is really impossible for you.**

Your value in God's eyes can be measured by the fact that He gave his son to die for you, to substitute you, to purchase a relationship with you. A price He would have willingly paid even if you were the only human on earth. Really, who in their right mind would decide to die for a worthless thing? Considering the price He paid for you, you must be worth zillions.

YOUR VALUE IN GOD'S EYES CAN BE MEASURED BY THE FACT THAT HE GAVE HIS SON TO DIE FOR YOU.

Unlike a cycling race where cyclists compete against each other; **The race of life is between you and yourself,** because you and you alone are equipped for your specific assignment and no one else.

Only you are equipped to fulfil your unique purpose, no one else will do it on your behalf. Your unique DNA code matches your purpose.
You are an authentic design, durable and robust.
You are a genuine brand. You were designed with all features necessary to fit your designated purpose. **Only you can deliver in your designated purpose with a distinction**. You are quality, genuinely strong, engineered to succeed in your purpose.

LET GO YOUR LOW SELF ESTEEM

If Barbie the blue-eyed blonde doll is still alive, she must have gained a bit of weight by now, or developed some acne I don't know, or maybe she finally grew some grey hair. I was never sure how old she was, but since everyone is subject to body changes, she must have reshaped a bit. Barbie was very famous in her days. She seemed to have the admired figure and beauty. She was as cool as Bimbo. I don't know how she got so many fans to adore her, but she had a big effect, especially on young girls. Maybe she was consistently on diet pills. She probably had a couple of breast implants over her life time. She probably spent all her money and time on surgery fixing and repairing her body to stay admirable to her fans. I don't know. Anyway, she is just one in a million with her kind of beauty, but I wouldn't advise anyone to take her serious. I just wonder if she really loved herself in the same way her fans felt about her.

Self esteem of people who appreciate themselves is strong and healthy, but those who always criticise themselves destroy their own self confidence. If Barbie could speak for herself, she would tell us how well she appreciates herself. But sadly, she is only a doll.

Judge yourself correctly

Some cultures, usually eastern cultures confuse humility with low self esteem. In such cultures being shy is mistaken for humility and is admired. Whereas shyness is a symptom of low self esteem. Shyness is a symptom that indicates broken self confidence. Acting shy shows you have a problem with accepting yourself equal to other people. You diminish yourself because you feel undeserving. Let me assure you, that too can change. Being shy is not permanent. It is just the way you look at yourself in comparison to others.

Maybe you judge others as better than yourself. Maybe you judge others as more gifted or better looking than you. You probably feel that you are not good enough, not good looking or whatever negative opinion you hold about yourself. That is all an under estimation of the real you.
So what if you are not perfect?
Who on earth is perfect?

You deserve better, you are equal to all people. You are God's creation, a master piece, a co-creator with God.

There is something special about you that cannot be found in anyone else, just in you.

Never judge yourself by looking at your weaknesses. Always appreciating yourself, and be grateful for your strengths. If you start believing positive things about you, then your attitude towards life will brighten. Your shy feelings will disappear and a new sense of self worth will grow.

Accepting God's view of who you are is the first step to becoming free of the bondage of low self esteem. Accept yourself as worthy of God's love, believe you deserve to be loved by others and stop measuring yourself against other people. You are worth it! It is true you just have to believe it.

KEEP YOUR HEAD ABOVE THE FUSS

The United States president Barack Obama, the man with the most powerful position in the world is a story of a boy who believed in his own possibilities yet in reality he grew up in no perfect circumstances. As a child his family changed homes several times, something that naturally destabilises a child. He went to school in different education systems when his parents moved from Indonesian to USA. He lost his father in a car accident, was raised by his grandmother. He faced same the kind of fears and doubts as any other child in his situation. Being raised by his grandmother could have damaged his self belief but he chose to not allow his circumstances to dictate over his dreams. He may have grown up with a confused identity being born from a Kenyan father and an American mother but he was determined not to allow his background to damage his self esteem. Even when his school mates called him 'the skinny kid with a funny name', he was strong inside and determined to hold his head above the fuss.

If you can accept your past with all its imperfections and its bitter moments as being necessary to mould you and make you strong, you will be able to overcome the toughest situations that seek to challenge your future.

Stereotypes

Free yourself from limiting cultural and racial stereotypes. One of the problems in our society is all the divisions and social classifications that we grow under. Stereotypes of all kinds can cause severe damage in the confidence of those who are being stereotyped against, and influence a false sense of superiority of one group over another. Such stereotypes as; blonds are dumber, brunets are smarter, and all other similar beliefs are not founded on any facts, but since people believe them, they become self fulfilling prophecies. This can negatively affect the self esteem of blonds and give an artificial superiority to brunets. There are many similar unfounded limiting beliefs that bind people in restraint. How about these?

- ⊙ White people can't sing as good as black people. Another one;
- ⊙ Black people will always do well in Sport and Music but not in Science.
- ⊙ Asians can only succeed in Business but not in Sport. We just cannot go through all of them.

The common truth in all stereotypes is that - they become self fulfilling prophecies, and have an effect on one's performance and self worth.

TAKE A NEW LOOK AT YOURSELF

In the Japanese culture a cosmetic Mirror is apparently a significant object. It is believed to hold the power of Self knowledge. They believe that if you know yourself better, you will perform better. My friend Alizon who lived in Japan for 8 years tells me that in Japan it is a common practise to have a mirror facing you in the office as you work. Workers glance at the mirror once in a while to admire themselves, this improves self confidence. It is a common practice for workers to glance regularly at themselves when they speak over the phone, to enhance their conversation. I guess it makes good sense because we respond differently when we aware of our expressions. If you have ever watched yourself on a video, you notice things you can improve about yourself which you would otherwise ignore. If you ever walked down a street alongside a glass building and suddenly notice yourself on the glass wall, you immediately readjust your posture and correct your walk; that is the power of self awareness.

People's Opinions about you

It is psychologically proven that the opinions you hold about yourself were planted in you during childhood as early as age one. This means we grow up holding people's opinions about us which are not valid. Your true potential can be restrained underneath the negative opinions of others. You can't afford to go through life living in the shadows of people's opinions. You may not stop people from saying things, but you can be selective of what to accept and believe about yourself. If you are not careful, people can plant negative seeds in you even as an adult and kill your Confidence.

You cannot afford to let the seeds of purpose and potential suffer from such weed of opinions. **The whole world is waiting for the**

full realisation of your purpose on Earth. So set yourself free of people's opinions and rise to your full confidence.

Self Confidence

To excel in your purpose, you need to develop an unshaking self confidence.

Being self confident does not mean self worship, self confidence is a steadfast belief that you have a significant value, you deserve to be heard. It is a mentally strong conviction about who you are without being arrogant about it. It comes from self acceptance and appreciation.

Accepting self means appreciating what God has made you to be without needing approval from others, regardless of your imperfections. Everything you are in totality makes you a special portrait of God's image.

> *THE WHOLE WORLD IS WAITING FOR THE FULL REALISATION OF YOUR PURPOSE ON EARTH.*

Self confident people are not *flippant*, they do not undermine other people. To the contrary they have respect for others, yielding where necessary yet keeping a firm position of self belief.

To be self confident is believing that you are worth being listened to, you deserve being taken seriously because you have a contribution to make.

Self confidence is attractive. Uncommon Achievers are well groomed and self confident people. You see their confidence in the way they carry themselves;

- ⊙ They look vibrant and vivacious.
- ⊙ They are cheerful and full of life.
- ⊙ They walk purposefully with great energy.
- ⊙ They speak with a clear, firm yet polite tone of voice.
- ⊙ They make other people feel important, at ease and welcomed in their presence.

Confidence is a powerful force;

- ⊙ Self Confidence inspires people around you,
- ⊙ Confidence enforces certainty over your dreams and
- ⊙ Confidence displays quality about you.

CHAPTER FOUR // DISCOVER AND NUTURE YOUR PERSONAL GENIUS

DISCOVER YOUR STRENGTHS

Can you believe that sweetness is in the sugar? That sounds rhetoric, but it illustrates the following point; You don't buy white powder and then add sweetness to make it sugar. You buy sugar for its sweetness and it happens to be a white powder. If you carelessly bought any white powder hoping it is sugar you would get a lot of surprises. Similarly, **you were born naturally gifted for your purpose like sweetness is to sugar.**

Your strengths are coded inside of you from birth; you were designed for your mission in life. Sugar and sweetness is object and its function and the two are synonymous just like you and your purpose. You are talented and endowed with strengths that are uniquely blended for your purpose.

Everyone is talented but what differentiates people is how they use their talents. Each an every person comes loaded with talents that are specific to help them function within their purpose.

You are never limited by lack of talent, but by lack of vision, by poor self knowledge and by neglecting your potential.

CONNECT WITH YOUR STRENGTHS

Your natural strengths also called *'signature strengths'* can be groomed and made fit to serve in your purpose. When blended well and sharpened, they can significantly increase your value as a person and your performance in your designated field of work.

Can you recall what your friends or parents usually say you are good at?

Have you ever had a friend say to you;

> "You are so good with people, you just make everyone feel comfortable in your presence."

It could be you have never really noticed this about yourself. To you chatting up people and making them feel good is just effortless, it comes naturally without a struggle. The reason you have never recognised this about yourself is because you think - everyone is good with people, its no big deal. To you working with people is a *'signature strength'* but for someone else it takes working on it and practice. Recognising your own strengths is the start to unlocking your greater life.

Whatever it is that you can do effortlessly, don't ignore it, treasure it, cultivate it, focus on it and prepare it, it will make a way for you to greatness.

Know your Inherited Strengths

It helps to understand your cultural strengths and family strengths. It makes it easy to figure out which strengths you are likely already good at. For an example; In a study published by Google to identify work-related and social strengths of certain nationalities, among others they found that Polish people were hard working people, some historic reasons must have contributed in shaping their values. The Germans are considered to be resilient, South Africans as musical, Philipinos are known for their hospitality, Jamaicans as good athletes and so on. Though some of the profiles from Google's report were obviously based on geographic advantages but understanding the strengths of your own nationality and culture can give you an advantage in specialising your talents. The blending of your natural talents and the skills learnt from social upbringing make you uniquely talented.

There is something you can do better than anybody else in the whole world. There is something that classes you as the cut above the rest.

DEVELOP YOUR UNIQUE TALENTS

Going back to your pet dog Skippy; If Skippy is a healthy dog, then he enjoys barking at suspicious strangers, running after your attention, chewing a bone and doing all sorts of stuff that dogs do. Let us say you also have a Parrot that is keen on learning new words, echoing your phrases and probably imitating your accent. You probably watch Skippy tilt his head looking enviously at the Parrot wishing he could also say a word or two. Actually it wouldn't be a bad idea for Skippy to speak, since he is more likely to go out shopping with you and meet people, instead of just woofing about in dog language. However learning a new language is one of Skippy's weaknesses, though gifted at sniffing up suspicious substances and doing all of the dog duties mentioned earlier. You would not want to waste your time and effort teaching English to Skippy, it would be a wasteful exercise but you can sharpen the abilities he is already good at, such as sniffing substances and playing.

You are of course not comparable with Skippy, but you too have both strengths and weaknesses. You are naturally more gifted on certain things than others. You do certain things effortlessly but also are inherently weak on certain things. **Your effectiveness lies on your dominant strengths not on your weaknesses.** Your dominant strengths hold the key to your success and efficiency.

If you prepare your dominant strengths adequately instead of developing your weaker abilities, you will enhance your effectiveness. If you work on your strengths daily, with time they will;

- ⊙ Increase your impact, your speed, and productivity
- ⊙ Give you a Power performance
- ⊙ Give you dominion over your work than if you tried to improve your weaknesses.

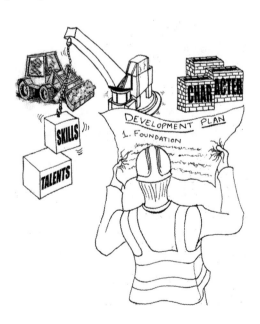

The X-Factor

Developing your dominant strengths, talents, skills will also increase your influence in your career, in relationships and your field of work. Your aim should be to master your strongest talents and skills not to develop your weaknesses, unless your weaknesses have a regressive effect on your strengths. You are already gifted with a unique combination of strengths that match your purpose, because of this; you have no business trying to develop your weaknesses. Remember you will always have some weaknesses, you are not perfect but you are complete.

YOUR EFFECTIVENESS LIES ON YOUR DOMINANT STRENGTHS NOT ON YOUR WEAKNESSES.

You are gifted with unique abilities which make you rare, special, something that separates you from everyone else in the world. The unique combination of your strengths gives you an X-factor, a special, uncommon effect that sets you apart. Your duty is to appreciate your X-factor, develop it and use it to your advantage. It is your X-factor that will make you stand out from the crowd. It is this X-factor that makes other people become interested in you. They are attracted to you because it makes you special, unique, and they ignore you when your X-factor is dull, diluted by trying to be someone you are not. Because everyone has an X-factor, then everyone should be attractive, especially when they embrace their X-factor.

There is something special about you, when you embrace it the world will be at your door step begging for it.

REFINE YOUR X-FACTOR

Your goal should be to refine your X-factor. Instead of wasting energy envying someone else's talents you are better embracing your own, working on them day by day until they are ready for premier use.

The difference between an expert and a mediocre is that the expert continues to refine their X-factor while the mediocre is simply satisfied.

1. **Take time to learn from people** who have mastered similar talents you want to develop, learn how they developed their talents. Make it easy for yourself, don't reinvent the learning process, just follow in their steps until you are happy with your progress, soon your unique strengths will shine prominently.

2. **Read Books** and Magazines relating to your talents. These days there are Magazines available in virtually every Field, from Cooking, to Designing Fashion, to playing Golf, to Investing in the Stock Market, and so on. Information will give you the Edge you need to become an Expert.

3. **Practice your Skill** diligently until your make a pro of yourself. A refined skill will bring you favour with people in senior positions. It will bring you before authorities, VIPs and open doors for you in high places. A refined Skill can even make you famous. For some fields, to get access to breakthrough opportunities and relevant knowledge a geographic shift is necessary. For instance; if you want to be an astronaut, you are better relocating to a country that is running a space program.

SPECIALISE YOUR SKILLS

Specialising your skills effectively requires narrowing down your talents to one or two or three talents at the most. Choose no more than three talents that you can focus on, just one is ideal. Do this by eliminating talents that you are weak at.

Waste no time on talents that you are not strong at. Give your **total focus** to the talent that comes easiest, also called *'core genius'*. Everyone has a natural talent. When developing your core genius, you may need to also develop one or two supportive skills. No one talent is without supportive skills. A writer is also a reader, a teacher is also a story teller, and so on. It is during the building of your talent that you discover which supportive skills you need. The demand for one skill over the other helps you decide where you can focus more of your energies.

INVEST IN YOUR GROWTH

1. Invest in yourself by attending courses that will empower you to be effective in your purpose.

2. Read relevant information; books, magazines, newsletters from the leaders in your field. Collect free articles from the internet.

3. Listen to relevant radio programs, and TV programs.

4. Read Success Stories especially Biographies of those who are significant in your field. Read about how they became successful and take Clues. Be specific in the type of information your spent your time on. It must relate to your particular purpose. If you are an Engineer, it's no use reading

about the sex life of mosquitoes; that cannot add any value to your engineering career.

As you accumulate knowledge in the area you want to be expert at, your own ideas will shape up to form a meaningful expertise. You will begin to understand exactly what you want to achieve in your field. You will have questions in mind such as, - Why didn't someone think of doing this to make things work better? As you notice such gaps, work out ways to resolve them, and soon you will realise that the areas uncovered were actually left for you to cover. Some of such gaps have never been covered since creation. This will make you a History Maker in your field.

Your Contribution to the World

You have in you the potential to bring new life in your field of calling.

Remember, you were created to be creative, to be a source of new ideas, to extend God's creative work on Earth with new innovations, to dominate and to be a co-creator with God. **Your creative contribution to the world is your service to God.**

It is important that you see yourself as a separate entity from your talents. You are not your talents. Your talents are the service you give and you are the servant. Be clear about your position; people are interested in the service not so much in the agent. One is the dish and the other is the meal. You are the casserole and your talent is the irresistible, tongue wetting yummy pudding in the casserole. People may like you, but it is really your service they appreciate about you. People like an empty beautiful casserole but they certainly can't resist a casserole loaded with good stuff. If the food tastes as good as the casserole looks, then that becomes the preferred dish for special occasions. Such is the relationship between you and your talent.

YOUR CREATIVE CONTRIBUTION TO THE WORLD IS YOUR SERVICE TO GOD.

USE IT OR LOSE IT

Let us look again at the parable of the talents in Matthew 25 verse 16. The third Steward who failed to invest his portion of money made his Master very furious. The angry Master commanded the man to give up his one portion and give it to the Steward with ten talents because he had invested his original five talents to make ten. Therefore he deserved to get more for being productive. The Master called the man who failed to invest his one talent, - a lazy, irresponsible, negligent, wicked man, because he had failed to grow what had been given to him in good faith. The Master didn't expect him to shelve the gift, he expected him to use it hence the Master decided he does not deserve to have anything.

You are a Steward of all the abilities that God has entrusted to you. You will be called to account for each talent that you have not used. To them that much has been given, much is expected.

In Physiology the term *atrophy* is used to describe dying of a muscle or organ due to lack of use. **Whatever is neglected will finally die.** Whatever is unused will finally waste away and atrophy. This of course includes talents, abilities, spiritual gifts, skills and any other thing that has life in it, and anything that has the potential to grow can also die.

WHATEVER IS NEGLECTED WILL FINALLY DIE, WHATEVER IS UNUSED WILL FINALLY WASTE AWAY AND ATROPHY.

The Snowball Effect

My Scottish friend Helen used to say;

"Keep your snowball rolling".

She usually said this referring to my talents and career. Initially this expression made no sense to me because in South Africa we don't play with snow, we don't get any.

One day as she said it again I asked her;

"What's with this rolling a snowball, I don't get it."

She replied;

"If you keep your snowball rolling, it gets larger and larger but as soon as you hold it, it starts to melt right there on your hands."

This is the Snowball Effect.

CHAPTER FIVE // DEVELOP AN UNCOMMON PURPOSE DRIVEN ATTITUDE

YOUR ATTITUDE WILL EITHER ATTRACT OR REPEL PEOPLE

Attitude is the way you respond to life and to everything that happens to you. Attitude is determined by how you **interpret** events and situations you run into daily especially those outside of your control, and how you interpret other people's interactions with you. How you **respond** to the events, situations and people determines your Character; the stuff you are made of.

I write this paragraph sitting at a public library on a two sitter desk. When I arrived at the desk, there was a young lady I found already seated at one end of the desk. Her books were scattered messily all over the desk, so I gently asked;

> "Excuse me, I wonder if I can use this side of the table please?"

I was expecting a response like;

> "Sure no problem, sorry about the mess, let me move the books out of the way."

Instead I got a blasting;

> "Can't you see I am using this desk. There are other desks in this library instead of you choose to come and harass me here... yari, yari, yari, yari..."

I tilted my head back in shock and I softly protested;

> "I am sorry but this desk is actually reserved and designated for laptop users and you are not using one. And it happens to be the only designated desk available, I'm only asking to use this end for my laptop, I'm sure we can share the desk."

To this she yelled even louder;

> "blah blah blah blah.... you come here thinking you can just push me around, and you blah blah blah blah blah blah..."

Fearing that yelling will interrupt other library users, I immediately walked away to get a librarian to take care of the situation, meanwhile she was pushing furniture violently and leaving the desk in explosive fury. As I settled down to work I couldn't stop thinking; just what happened to good old character? Where did it go wrong? With all this talk about us being a better empowered generation yet we still display the manners of animals.

Humility

Our personal insecurities show up so fast as soon as we feel cornered into uncomfortable situations. We get agitated, feel attacked, and take on an aggressive defence, and quickly want to prove that we don't deserve to be humble. Humility is a virtue we all hate because it brings us down to the level of everyone else. It demotes us from our self held superiority and strips us off our delusions of self-importance. Meanwhile, if we held an attitude of humility we would gain favour with other people, and even attract the favour of God. According to the Bible, God resists the proud, but gives grace to the humble. The Bible also says considering others greater than yourself is the true sense of greatness.

Whether your Attitude is good or bad, it shines brighter than your own eyes can see, it shouts louder than you think, it is so glamorous that people remember it longer than they remember your talents.

People may forget what you were wearing but they won't forget how you conducted yourself. **Your Attitude will either attract people to you or push them away.**

Becoming a Person of Integrity

Integrity is what you give in exchange for a good reputation, so consistency matters.

If you think you are a nice person, no one else knows that about you until they experience your being nice. To people you are not kind until you have acted kind. Their experience of you is what counts not what you think about yourself. What you imagine yourself to be, exists only in your head, it only leaves other people to decide what kind you are. The problem is their opinion will likely discredit you, so it is your responsibility to present yourself as the character that reflects your true worth. Be fair to yourself, be consistent, be sincere, be true to who you are.

Once you have decided to be morally good, the true test of character is doing what you believe is right even when no one can seen your goodness. **Personal integrity is always tested in the dark corner that has no witness.**

Once you have decided to be an honest person, it is self defeating to add a few white lies just because it is convenient. Any true virtue gets tested for endurance. Whether you are honest or not, it will be revealed in the moment of pressure when a little white lie seems to be the perfect option. Mind you, we all lie at some point, but to grow in integrity you need to have enough commitment to stand by the truth regardless how popular or unpopular it is.

In relationships you don't get what you want, you get what you are. Even though your talent can open new doors and introduce you to friends in high places, but what will keep you there is character.

In general people are attracted to an easy going down to earth character. People enjoy a genuine person, yet once they discover one lie from you, they are more likely not to believe anything you say again in future and even question the integrity of things you said in the past. Besides, to maintain just a single lie can be such a busy jumble, because for every lie you say you need at least five more lies to cover it, and to protect your reputation you have to remember all your previous lies just in case something does not add up.

IN RELATIONSHIPS YOU DON'T GET WHAT YOU WANT, YOU GET WHAT YOU ARE.

Considering that we are not perfect, we are consistently going through shaping as an act of God moulding us. We are creatures and he is the creator. We therefore have a right to ask Him for help to strengthen us in character. When you involve God in your affairs He will work in you to express through you His greater purposes, just to show off his magnificence through you. God takes a personal responsibility in shaping us up for our destiny, when we ask him to get involved. Once he starts a good work in you, you can trust him to work it through to completion. (Phil 1:6)

BUILD CHARACTER PLUS

> Suppose you went to a friend's house at midnight, wanting to borrow three loaves of bread. You would say to him, 'A friend of mine has just arrived for a visit, and I have nothing for him to eat.' He would call out from his bedroom, 'Don't bother me. The door is locked for the night, and we are all in bed. I can't help you this time.' But I tell you this—though he won't do it as a friend, if you keep knocking long enough, he will get up and give you what you want so his reputation won't be damaged. - (Luke Chapter 11 Verse 5-8; New Living Translation)

This is a story of determination and persistence of a neighbour who just refuses to quit. Though the friend initially holds on to his pillow hoping the knock at the door will eventually go away, but because of the neighbour's unshaken determination, refusing to take 'no' for an answer he could no longer resist but get up and give the neighbour all he wanted. **Determination accompanied by faith and persistence knows no limits.**

Determination

One of my favourite cartoon characters is Pink Panther; he is a real '*die hard*'. To me he is the master of determination. On all his assignments there is always some enemy waiting at some corner to deter him from finishing his assignment. If it's not the nasty dog from the neighbourhood waiting to chew his pink tail, then it's the brutal gunman waiting to spray bullets into his thin frail body. But, is he ever deterred? If Pink Panther is attacked on his first attempt, he simply runs for cover and if he survives, which he always does. He gets up and gets back on his mission with even more determination and enthusiasm, attempting new ways to get to his target. He is always determined to try as many times as it takes for his attacker to get tired and give up. Finally his opposer inevitably gets tired and lets him pass, but for Pink Panther giving up is never an option.

Pink Panther will do whatever it takes to complete his assignment. He never takes 'no' for an answer. He has never failed a single mission. He doesn't know what it means to quit. It may take him longer to accomplish some missions but his tenacity always pays off. He just never says 'die'.

A marathon runner once described his running mate as having *'class'*. Describing what he meant by class, he explained;

"I love pacing myself to this guy because he has the ability to call on reserved energy during the toughest time in the race. During a marathon we all hit an invisible barrier like an invisible wall, when legs just can't take it anymore. From that point on it's not the muscle that completes the race, it's the character. Some runners have speed but lack the determination that is required by the race."

The race of life also requires more than just speed, it calls for internal strength. Uncommon Achievers have the determination and the commitment to overcome any number of challenges during their race, and break every wall to reach the finishing line.

A person with determination still gets tired and weary but how they respond to the temptation of that moment makes all the difference. For them feeling tired is an indication that it is time to gear into reserved energy. Determination doesn't mean you never get tempted to quit, but it means you never actually quit. Runners of a race are most tempted to slow down in the final stages of the race just when the finishing line is only few metres away, and this is where determination counts the most. Determination is the single minded focus to touch the finishing line with the same passion as from the start.

An African elder famous for his wisdom one day had a boy visit him for advice. The boy asked him;

> "I would like to know what you think is the number one secret for success in life."

The old man looked at the young man's eyes and said nothing, testing him to see if he was genuine. The boy persisted, persuading the old man to say something;

> "I have come a long way to talk to you, I will not go without an answer, its fine if you can't talk right now I will wait, I have all the time in the world to hear your advice."

Realising the boy was serious the old man stood up held the boy by the hand and led him down to a river nearby. As they walked side by side, no one said a word. The young man was wondering in anticipation for a reply but the old man just kept walking. They walked into the water knee-deep, then waist-deep, and then completely underwater. The old man just kept going with his hand tightly clenched on the boy's wrist, meanwhile the boy battled for breath trying to free his hand but the old man would not let go his hand. Minutes later, the old man finally led him out of the water desperate for air. For the first time the old man opened his mouth and asked;

> "Have you found it?"

"Find what, you old fool! You almost killed me!" Upset the boy replied.

"Have you found the number one secret for success in life?" The old man asked.

"The only thing I've found is that you are mad and you know nothing." The boy shouted.

"You see, if you want success in life as desperate as you wanted to breathe in that water when I held your hand, and if you are as determined as you were determined to get out of my grip, you will certainly find success."
The old wise man made his point.

In the famous story of Jacob in Genesis 32, it was sheer determination that made Jacob wrestle with an angel all night long, and would not let go the angel without getting a blessing. Even when Jacob had already dislocated his hip in the fight, he latched on, determined not to let go until the angel had no choice but bless him.

FIGHT WITH TENACITY

There are times when you just feel like you have tried enough, you have given life everything you've got, now you have nothing more to give. You feel like you have exhausted all your internal resources; you have run out hope, patience, energy and motivation to go on. This is when perseverance counts the most, this is when perseverance can be best exercised, to go through such times calls for internal toughness.

In hard situations such as dealing with failure, rejection, breaking an addiction, tragedy, extreme poverty, loss of a loved one and other discouraging situations that override human reasoning, it takes more than just natural strength to persevere. It calls for supernatural intervention. It is good to know that God has actually promised to intervene to give you strength at the time of need, if you ask him for help. God will give you strength and the grace to go on when you need it most. Just ask.

Sometimes life can get so hard that even getting up after a long night sleep is an effort. If you have ever been through this, you will know the feeling of waking up feeling weary, too tired to face another day, feeling so drained so much that even lifting your head off the pillow is an effort. It's a feeling you wouldn't want to experience. You know you are not physically sick, but you are sick of living. You have tried all you can and nothing motivates you to get up and try anymore.

If this book finds you in such a state of feeling as if you have reached the bottom, if it helps you find new strength to rise and pursue your dream, then it has fulfilled my mission. It was worth the effort just for you. I have myself had moments where I reached my bottom, and to your surprise; this book is a product of such a time, - a moment of feeling empty, just wanting to give it all up. **But I decided long ago to die trying than to give up**.

Persistence

Never stop pushing.
Never stop trying.
Never give up.

When you feel you have given it all, get up and give a little bit more.

Try it from a new angle.

Just keep trying. Don't stop.

Refuse to give in or give up.

Keep trying like a mad man, as if your life depends on it.

Don't let go, sustain your hope until winning becomes possible.

When things go wrong as they do sometimes, and your journey seems all uphill, when your resources run low and challenges are high, when you want to smile but feel cast down, just tell yourself it is not time to quit.

If uncertainties bring you many twists and turns and your progress has slowed down to zero, just keep telling yourself it is not yet time to give up.

During those faint moments often the goal is nearer than it seems. The darkest hour is the one before dawn. It is always too early to give up. Just keep going.

I once read a story of miners who worked for months digging a mine which they believed held treasures of gold, but after months of trying and getting nothing, they grew tired of hoping and gave up. Though they knew geological tests had indicated that the mine definitely has gold, but the joy of trying was gone. So they decided to sell the mine obviously making losses from the months of working and getting nothing in return. The new mining company that bought the mine dug for few meters and to their surprise there appeared what seemed like an endless supply of gold. Often when we are at the point of giving up, we are only few meters away from success.

You may be familiar with the old story of Thomas Edison the inventor of the light bulb who became famous for his resilience and obviously for inventing the light bulb. After he had failed five thousand times to make the bulb work, a journalist asked him why he bothered to keep trying after failing five thousand times already. Because Mr Edison believed he was no quitter, he answered;

> "You may think I have failed five thousand times but I believe I have learnt five thousand ways to avoid when creating a light bulb."

Of course with that kind of determination he finally got the light bulb to work. But just imagine the world without light bulbs had Mr Edison given up. Success is guaranteed to the uncommon person who is will be resilient and diligent in their pursuit.

Having a persevering character has the similar effect as carbon has on steel. Carbon makes steel unbreakable. It gives it a strength that does not fail under pressure. It may bend, but it just won t break.

When facing testing times, which is inevitable, your guarantee to overcome is if you persevere through. To give up is to invite complete defeat.

If you really want to see victory, the first thing to do is never talk defeat, instead affirm your success. Once you speak defeat, you are accepting failure. Avoid using words that will exhaust your energy such as;

> "I'm just wasting my time trying." Or
> "I can't see what I'm doing."

Don't even allow a thought of defeat or doubt, if you do; you will be letting yourself become vulnerable to defeat. You will be accepting defeat before it even occurs. Why exhaust yourself when you can exalt yourself. Uncommon Achievers use self-talk to reaffirm their victory even before they see signs of victory. They say words like;

> "I believe I can and I will!"
> "It may be tough right now but victory is certain!"

CHAPTER SIX // ALIGN YOURSELF WITH PURPOSE CENTRED SUCCESS

TUNE IN TO THE SUCCESS FREQUENCY

Just like a Radio Station, you've got to be in the right frequency to get success. Success does not come randomly by chance, it comes as a result of a correct combination of actions. Like Radio frequencies, it is always available and ready for whoever is willing to tune in and connect to the right frequency. Your duty is to align your actions to the success frequency by adjusting four factors;

❶ Your **Thoughts**
❷ Your **Words**
❸ Your **Habits** and
❹ Your **Associations**

Success comes by attraction, it does not come from a random aimless increase of effort or extra hard work trying to succeed. You must be correctly positioned for success first. Then success will come. It is attracted by a correct combination of four things;

❶ The Things you think about.

❷ The Words you use.

❸ The Habits you do daily.

❹ The kind of People you associate with.

Just like trying to make fire using an *Optical magnifying glass*; it will only burn your pieces of paper when you get two things right; the correct angle and the correct distance where sun rays are most concentrated towards your paper. You can fiddle all day with the optical magnifier and get nothing even though the sun is shining bright, unless the sun rays are beamed at a correct combination of both the angle and the distance only then will you get fire.

Only when **your mindset** (thoughts), **your language** (words), **your lifestyle** (habits) and **your environment** (associations) are adjusted correctly to attract success will you succeed. Then you will attract and cause such an explosion of success like you can never achieve with any amount of random hard work.

To become an Uncommon Achiever, these four traits are the essential recipe you should focus on;

❶ **A Winning Mindset which is driven by a Positive Attitude, and that can only come by thinking Positive Thoughts.**

❷ **A Correct Language of Success, which can only come from speaking Words of Faith and Positive Talk.**

❸ **A Success Oriented Lifestyle, and this can only be achieved by practising Success Habits daily.**

❹ **And being in a Success-Inciting Environment, meaning spending time with people who talk success and promote success.**

Once you get this combination right, your life will attract so much success exceeding any other effort you can ever try to get success.

First you need to make it your personal responsibility to succeed, avoid shifting blame for any past or current failures, then work on yourself gradually developing the four success traits discussed above until you reach an outburst of success. Every success habit such as speaking positively, managing time, setting goals, working well with people, can all be learned, practiced and mastered.

Once you start building a pattern of good habits, keep that routine until your mind forms an **unbreakable rhythm**. Research indicates that we are likely to accept a new pattern of habits as a lifestyle if it has been repeated for 30 days without breaks. Your rhythm should include a series of daily activities that when done together give you results, that will become your **personal productive rhythm**. The value of each activity must be based on its purpose, - why do you have to do this activity? From the time you get up, your plan is to accomplish something not to just fill the day with activities but to accomplish results. Your plan should be to **standardise your daily routine,** by doing specific productive actions daily until you get results. Repeat the same pattern until your body and mind accept it as your new lifestyle. Always put God at the driving seat of your plans, he will guide you in the path of success and make your journey a productive one. (Prov 16:3)

THE HABIT OF ORGANISING YOUR THOUGHTS

If thoughts were clothes and you had to wear something everyday, you would be careful what you wear. You would wear clothes suitable for the weather and for each occasion. For a cold weather, you would dress warm. For a hot day out at the beach you would put on a swimming costume, and save your formal wear for the evening banquette. We are selective about what we wear, we manage our clothes to make sure we feel good, we attract respect and we look presentable. This is because we know that clothes don't just cover the body, they have a meaning. They make an impact, they have consequences too when used wrongly. If you got up and carelessly picked something off the shelf and dumped it on you and rushed out of the house without a care how you look, you can expect to see shock on people's faces or worse of become a laughingstock. Perhaps even the weather would punish you for your negligence. However we don't do that, we properly manage what we wear because we are fully aware of the **consequences** and the **responsibility** that goes with wearing wrong clothes.

Thoughts ought to be managed just like clothes, **because thoughts also have Effects, Outcomes and Consequences.**

Thoughts are causes and the Conditions in your life are the Effects.

Thoughts can be projected towards specific outcomes and conditions. For instance;
- ⊙ Happy thoughts bring Happiness.
- ⊙ Thoughts dominated by Fear bring Defeat and reduce Self Confidence.
- ⊙ Thoughts of Failure attract Failure.

⊙ Positive thoughts bring Positive Outcomes.

⊙ Expectations of Victory enforce Victory.

⊙ Thoughts of prosperity attract Wealth, and so on.

The current conditions in your life today are the outcomes of your thoughts. Where you are today is due to the kind of thoughts that have dominated your mind in the last few months or years.

Just like clothes, if you are negligent about what goes through your mind, you can expect shocking results. **However you can choose what to think about depending on what you want to see in your future.**

Where you will be few months from now depends on the kind of thoughts that will dominate your mind from now on. In life you don't get what you wish for, you get what you consistently think about.

You attract into your life the resources, the people, the situations and conditions that are in line with your dominant thoughts. Your life as it is now reflects your present and past thoughts, so changing your thoughts will change your future.

Whatever dominates your thoughts will continue to grow and increase and finally dominate your life.

Both bad and good things are the products of thoughts. From now on you will have what you allow into your thoughts. Think of yourself as a magnet drawing to you the conditions, resources, situations and people according to your dominant thoughts. The recipe for great and exciting conditions is to keep your thoughts, imaginations and expectations on exciting things, things you want to see in your future and even better on the promises of God.

WHATEVER DOMINATES YOUR THOUGHTS WILL CONTINUE TO GROW AND INCREASE AND FINALLY DOMINATE YOUR LIFE.

Creative Thinking

If you want something in the future, start dominating your mind with thoughts as you would have it. If your desire is to have children in the future, instead of dominating your thoughts with your current reasons for not having children, start dominating your thoughts as things would be when you already have children. Imagine yourself playing swing with your future daughter, and allow no doubt in your mind to take this picture away. By doing so, you strengthen your faith and expectation. If having a happy family is important to you, then attract this condition by planting thoughts of you enjoying happy moments with your family. The same principle applies to finances, opportunities, houses, cars, hopes, dreams and desires.

Thoughts give birth to things, and thoughts are a powerful tool you can use to craft the future you want.

You can use thoughts to project a successful career, material things you want to own, relationships you want to have, and even project the role you desire to play in your field of work.

Thoughts are seeds, your mind is the garden, you are the farmer, the conditions in your life are fruits of all you think about, and you decide what harvest you will reap by the seeds you plant.

If you dominate your mind with thoughts of excellence, you will reap fruits of excellence and nothing less. Your mind delivers results that are consistently in line with your dominant thoughts. You can transform your life by renewing your thoughts, aligning them with excellence, with scripture, with quality things and with positive expectations. (Romans 12:2) Whatever is of good quality, whatever is excellent, whatever is profitable, whatsoever is lovely and of virtue think on these things (Philippians 4:8).

Proverbs chapter 23 verse 7 says; as a man thinks in his heart, so is he. **So we don't only get what we think about, we also become what we think about**. The real you is what is projected in your thoughts.

As you think of yourself ultimately you become. If you think you are a smart career girl, attractive and likeable, you can be sure to get results from those thoughts. You can expect to see increase in your attractiveness, increase in likeability and respect in the way people treat you. The same effect applies in negative thoughts as well; Negative thoughts bring chaos, lack, rejection and every kind of negative condition. **From now on you will become as you think of yourself.**

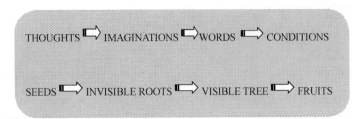

To get rid of unwanted thoughts takes quite an effort but is worth every effort. Since they were interlaced over a long period of time, they cannot just disappear overnight. It takes time to completely forget old thoughts because they are deeply embedded in the mind. You need to consistently substitute every unwanted thought with new thoughts until the old way of thinking fades away. It takes patience. **Thoughts don't just go away because they are no longer wanted unless they are replaced with new thoughts, and the same applies to unwanted habits.** Just like a cord of thin threads weaved tightly together, thoughts and habits become stronger each time they are repeated. With time they become unbreakable.

AS YOU THINK OF YOURSELF ULTIMATELY YOU BECOME.

THE HABIT OF SPEAKING WHAT YOU WANT

This is a habit of Faith. Just like thoughts words possess the key to our future. They are a trigger to life or to death, they have both creative and destructive potential. If God used words to create the universe, that means everything around us both visible and invisible were once words in the mouth of God. The same power that created the earth and everything in it is in you, in your words, in your mouth.

With your words you can create, bring new life and new things.

With your words you can activate new situations and activate the promises of God.

With your words you can also destroy, condemn and terminate negative situations.

> "The tongue has the power of life and death, and those who love it will eat its fruit". (New International Version; Proverbs Chapter 18 Verse 21).

What You Say Is What You Get (WYSI-WYG). You can use words to your advantage or against yourself. Using the power of words you can talk yourself to good life, inasmuch as you can speak words of defeat and self destruct. So if words are so creative, then you can be wise to say only what builds, encourages, and uplift yourself and others instead of using them to tear down or condemn.

You can use the creative power of words to affirm dreams that have not yet materialised until they materialise.

Faith

When you use words to affirm your expectations, you increase and strengthen your faith.

What is faith?
Faith is being sure of things we hope for and being confident about what we do not yet see as definitely coming. (Heb 11:1)

All creation that we see in the physical form comes from the formless, which is invisible. All creation came from the invisible power of words and faith.

Our words are seeds to things to come which are presently in their formless status. When our words are mixed with an unshaken faith, a confident expectation that we will certainly get what we expect, then the results become definite. Strong belief is the backbone of faith and faith in its nature is a force that never fails. Confident faith is able to bring to life a dying dream, it can turn a situation that is heading for disaster into a celebration.

Faith is made alive and triggered to action by the expression of our words.

Faith speaks the confidence that you actually have it already what you are expecting. (Mark 11:24)

Just like thoughts, you don't get only what you say you also become what you say about yourself. Take a look at your life right now; it is filled with evidence of your words. You are experiencing self fulfilling prophecies from your own mouth. You are right now experiencing all the things you have been saying about yourself. You have influenced situations into your life both good and bad knowingly or unknowingly.

YOU DON'T GET ONLY WHAT YOU SAY YOU ALSO BECOME WHAT YOU SAY ABOUT YOURSELF.

What we speak is usually what we sincerely believe about ourselves and ultimately becomes the direction we are going. To get uncommon results you just have to speak out of faith rather than speak based on the facts that are currently challenging your life, especially if your current situation is not a good one. By faith declare things like;

"I am fruitful and getting better everyday"

"I am prosperous with an overflowing surplus to help others"

Say it even if your wallet is hungry right now simply because you understand the creative power of your words.

Begin a powerful habit of talking to yourself. Influence your life with your words. Start a habit of speaking life giving words to yourself;

- Speak words of Hope
- Speak words of Strength
- Invite Favour
- Decree your own Victories
- Speak Excellence
- Speak yourself to Health
- Command Prosperity

And your life will overflow with these things.

Things have ears, they will respond to you if you speak with Faith and Confidence.

Socially, we also become as we speak; If you speak with words of authority, people's confidence in you grows, giving you the power of leadership. Just as well if you speak out of defeat or out of fear and self pity you invite people to walk all over you.

Negative talk demoralises, discourages and has disastrous effects. If you are experiencing negative conditions right now, that is evidence and manifestation of your negative talk. Words become self fulfilling prophecies.

If you are going to speak anyway, why not use words to bless yourself, to influence your dreams, to activate God's promises, and develop a language that brings you success not failure.

You can change your life by changing your words; and you can change your words by changing your beliefs. But remember now since your beliefs are the product of your thoughts it means you need to change your thoughts first. And surround yourself with positive speaking people because **what you hear determines what you will believe**. Our beliefs are formed and influenced by the people we spend most time with.

Indulging in a negative language is dangerous for your whole soul. Avoid words like;
> "I can't"
> "Not me"
> "It's too difficult"
> "It's impossible"
> "I'm a failure"

They are self destructing words and damage your confidence and expectation.

Rather use words like;
> "I can"
> "Why not"
> "No problem"
> "I'll do my best".

There is no earthly acceptable reason to justify the use of the statement "*I can't*", it is the most cruel way to paralyze your potential. It stops you from considering any possibilities. Always believe in yourself because you can do all things with your God given ability, and when your ability fails, God will give you strength to go the extra mile if you ask for it. His strength is made perfect when our strength fails. With his strength you will overcome any size of challenge.

IF YOU ARE GOING TO SPEAK ANYWAY, WHY NOT USE WORDS TO BLESS YOURSELF, TO INFLUENCE YOUR DREAMS, TO ACTIVATE GOD'S PROMISES, AND DEVELOP A LANGUAGE THAT BRINGS YOU SUCCESS NOT FAILURE.

THE HABIT OF VISUALIZING YOUR GOALS

When I worked as a software programmer, before I could bend over my computer to write software I had to have a mental picture of the software I wanted to create. A client would relate a business problem that they wanted to solve, and I would have to create a mental picture of a fully functioning software that can solve that problem. In my mental picture, there would be menus, sub menus, buttons to click, data fields and every other detail. Then the next step was to interpret my mental images onto paper in form of diagrams and algorithms for the client to see, understand and approve. The images in my head were the *blue print* of what will be when the software is finally complete. Few weeks later when the software is complete, I would show to the client on the screen for the first time what I had already seen many times in my mind's eye since day one. This was visualisation at work.

A habit of visualising the finished product or your goal as already accomplished will accelerate the process of achieving it.

The mind serves us in two ways;

With **memory** - which is pictures from the past.

And with **imagination** - which is pictures from the future - things to come.

Visual Aids

Using Visual Aids is a popular idea with Uncommon Achievers. They keep pictures and posters of dream houses, dream cars, dream jet planes to help them stay focused towards their goals. They understand the importance of keeping a clear mental picture of the dream they want, until it materialises.

Visual Aids will strengthen your faith, your imagination, increase your expectations and help you stay in the right frame of mind regarding your dream or the future you desire.

Visual Aids will help you stay focused on what will become when your goal is finally accomplished. Generally we waste time being out of focus, sidetracked, demotivated and even depressed because we have lost the mental picture that got us motivated to pursue the goal at the beginning.

Collect photos that represent the dream you are pursuing to help you see where you are going. Put them visibly in your room, on the walls, in your office, in your wallet, use them as Visual Aids. Each time you see the picture it will revive your expectation and excitement as though your goal was already attained. This will enforce its achievement.

In Genesis chapter 30 there is a story of a man - Jacob who used Visual Aids to assist him get his goal; He wanted more spotted goats and black sheep to be born from Laban's flock of white sheep and plain goats. Jacob's boss Laban had cut a deal with Jacob that he would give him as wages every sheep that is born black and every goat that was born spotted. Laban's deal was based on a fact that there were simply no such goats or sheep in his flock so that Jacob would work for nothing. But in faith Jacob pealed few sticks from a poplar tree making spots on them and drilled them on the ground where the sheep would come for their daily drink. In his mind the sticks represented spotted goats and black sheep, the sticks helped him imagine a flock with mixed livestock instead of the current livestock with only white sheep and plain goats. Because of Jacob's faith, his expectation, assisted by his Visual Aids the sheep started a habit of mating at the river where his faith-sticks were drilled. This happened every time they came for a drink. They started producing a breed of spotted goats and black sheep more than ever witnessed by both Laban and Jacob. Jacob became so prosperous that his boss Laban became jealous.

If you are a couple trying out for a baby this story should give you ideas of the kind of pictures you should have in your bedroom walls.

You can bring to life whatever you are able to clearly imagine with an intense emotion as though it is already accomplished. It is not enough to just visualize it in the mind's eye, you must also feel the excitement as if you already own it and speak it with your mouth. Feel that emotional experience as though what you imagine is happening currently in real life. Using visualization will accelerate its accomplishment if you repeatedly visualize and emotionalise your goal until it sinks into your subconscious mind. And remember to keep your words and thoughts aligned with your expectations.

> *A HABIT OF VISUALISING THE FINISHED PRODUCT OR YOUR GOAL AS ALREADY ACCOMPLISHED, WILL ACCELERATE THE PROCESS OF ACHIEVING IT.*

The habit of Visualisation is also used to increase performance in work activities, music, drama and sports. Olympians, sport players and artists who use the process of visualization as part of their training routine claim to notice significant improvements in their actual performance when they have pre-run mental routines first.

THE HABIT OF DREAMING BIG

As children our inborn dream machine was fired up, ready to reach for the stars, undermining any limits, but as adults we grow to fear big ambitions in the name of "reality check". Kids dream the impossible. They think they can do anything and be anything they want. When you were a kid, you would see an athlete on TV and immediately put yourself in that picture doing it better. If there was a singer that impressed you, you felt the notes come from your own belly. You knew no limits. You dreamed without reservations. You counted no costs. You dreamed without limits.

You need to turn on your dream machine so that you can release your full potential. You need to be able to dream the impossible again as you did as a child. Learn to dream again, no one can teach you how to dream, you already have it inside of you. Release yourself, set high goals, dream big dreams, aim for the stars, dream without reservations.

Once a dream has been conceived inside of you, it will guide where your energies should flow. It will call your latent strengths to action. It will invoke the intelligence in you that has not been used yet.

Big dreams attract God's attention, blessings and favour.

Big dreams attract big measures of finances to match the demand.

The bigger your dream, the bigger you become as you pursue it.

Mark Shuttleworth the only African astronaut who has been to the moon, he had a dream to go to the moon but such a dream was too big and practically impossible under his conditions at the time. He kept his dream alive until one day at age 29 an opportunity availed itself when he sold an internet software program to a company and made enough to accomplish his dream. His dream made a way for him. Mark not only did he achieve his dream, he also gained recognition as one of the top achievers in his country South Africa. Big dreams attract recognition, big dreams attract new experiences, a big dream will connect you to people in high places. No dream is too big to be accomplished, only that bigger dreams demand bigger effort. The resources and opportunities available to you as up to now are proportional to the size of your dreams.

> *THE BIGGER YOUR DREAM, THE BIGGER YOU BECOME AS YOU PURSUE IT.*

Peter Daniels an Australian who travelled the world teaching on wealth creation became a Multi-Millionaire and very famous as he fulfilled his dream. He tells his personal story from being a poor bricklayer at age 26 to becoming so rich that even banks would borrow money from him. Peter Daniels is completely illiterate; he educated himself in his late twenties by reading a dictionary word to word, and asking people to help him with pronunciation. He had suffered most of his young life with a rare diesis called Diphtheria. Though Peter came from a disadvantaged and poor background he had a dream; something bigger than himself, he wanted to see how much wealth a person can accumulate during a lifetime and how much of it he can give away. As unusual as his dream was for a bricklayer, let alone poor and disadvantaged but he worked extremely hard to see his dream come to pass and he fulfilled much more than he had originally expected.

A great dream is the one that will help you grow as a person but also contribute to the lives of people around you. It helps if your dream is in line with your over all purpose in life. If you are interested in cars, then you will be more motivated pursuing a dream that involves cars such as hiring cars, or running a car dealership. For someone who loves kids, they will be motivated if they pursue a dream that involves children such as running a nursery or helping troubled children with shelter and welfare.

THE HABIT OF SPENDING TIME WITH SUCCESS MINDED PEOPLE

Birds of the same feather flock together to the same direction, to the same destiny and usually have the same purpose in mind. Your lifestyle and your persuasions reflect the type of company you keep. People who spend time together have;

- ⊙ Similar beliefs
- ⊙ Similar lifestyles
- ⊙ Similar attitudes
- ⊙ Similar perspective towards life.

Naturally everybody is influenced by the company they keep. The type of company you hang out with is a deciding factor whether you will succeed or not. If you are genuine about fulfilling your destiny, spent your time with people who are busy fulfilling their destiny. Associate with world changers, they will influence your thinking knowingly or unknowingly. **The most fertile environment for success is when you surround yourself with success driven people and Uncommon Achievers.**

Your limitations, the way you think and talk, your addictions and the risks you take are all influenced by your associations.

How far you will go in attempting to fulfil your dreams depends on the type of people you associate with. You are only as successful as someone else you already know.

If you are not happy with the level of your output, look at the people you spend time with, may be its time to change friends.

You cannot be an eagle flying with turkeys, it's impossible. **If you aspire to be an Eagle, then fly like an Eagle and definitely fly only with Eagles.**

A Farmer who raised a lion cub among his dogs, later discovered that his mighty pet had absolutely no clue of its mighty nature. It ate with dogs, played with dogs and even ran to hide when the dogs ran from danger.

> *IF YOU ASPIRE TO BE AN EAGLE, THEN FLY LIKE AN EAGLE AND DEFINITELY FLY ONLY WITH EAGLES.*

CHAPTER SEVEN // RECOGNISE AND PURSUE YOUR PURPOSE

YOUR PERSONAL SIGNS TO FOLLOW

The Secret to becoming an Uncommon Achiever is knowing your Purpose in Life. The Primary Pursuit and Focus of Uncommon Achievers is to fulfil their God given Purpose in Life.

Have you noticed that we dismiss things as useless when we don't know their function until one day we need them, then from that day their value changes from useless to essential. One day you have a problem, and to your surprise a solution comes from something you knew all the time but trivialised its potential, and suddenly its Purpose changes from worthless to very important.

A Problem is an opportunity to discover hidden Purposes.

Where there is a Problem, there is a potential to discover new purposes, new opportunities, new progress and new experiences. Your purpose as a person maybe hidden in a problem that has not found its solution yet, and the solution to that problem could be YOU.

Do you know of a problem that seems to attract your attention, a crisis that bothers you, or a situation that needs to be improved? May be you are exposed to a crises that affects a group of people in another country, or in your own country, such as some political or social injustice. Maybe it is a problem that is affecting your own family, such as 'poverty'. It is possible that you don't see yourself qualified to solve it, yet if you started to look at yourself as the solution, you would be surprised how events begin to unfold to your favour thereon. You would be surprised how people come to favour and support you and how resources start to come at the moment of need.

When you see yourself as a solution to a problem, then your purpose is at work. Purpose is simply the problem that gets your attention.

1. Is there a **Need** or **Problem** that stands out to you when you watch TV while others don't even take notice of it, something that tends to jumps into your face when you read News Papers. You hear people talk about it and it drives you mad that all they do is just talk about it instead of doing something. Does it move you enough to give your life to solve it? It could be you get mad at souls that die without knowing about Jesus, so you decide to do something about it, or some other need or problem.

2. Can you think of an **Idea** or **Activity** that wins your interest? Do you know people who would benefit from this idea if you gave your time to work on it? Do you care enough for these people to give your life to work on this Idea? Or are you persuaded enough of the benefits of this idea that you would

dare work on it with or without other people's support. It could be a Business Idea, Research Idea, Academic Concept, Political Idea, Social Change, the list goes on.

3. Are you passionate about a **Doctrine**, a **Principle** or some **Concept** that you can give your life to represent it? You need not worry about the platform to express your views. Simply work on the Concept, when it is refined an opportunity or platform will become available either through news paper, TV, radio program, by writing a book, live audience, internet or magazine, or a new group forming in support of your concept or belief.

4. Is there a **Service**, an **Assignment** or **Type of Work** you desire to do but you just haven't had the opportunity to do yet? You may even be downplaying it thinking you don't have what it takes to be good at it. You feel so passionate about it that you could do this work even without being paid for it, just because you love doing it. You could do it for the love of it if money was not a problem. It gives you a feeling like you shine when you do it. It could be working with children, animals, working with hair, plants, or something else specific.

5. Is there a **Type of Performance** or an **Activity** that fuels your ambitions, it could be a sport activity you go to bed and start dreaming ideas about. You feel given a chance, you would excel at it. It could be some art such as painting, playing music, singing, acting, storytelling, teaching, or photography.

6. Is there a certain **Type of People** you would like to work with? You find yourself attracted to this kind of people; there is a connection you can't even explain that draws you to them. You have a strong desire to do something for them. It could be some type of children, or some tribe or race that

you want to help. It could be just to help the local youth in your area.

7.   Your Assignment and Purpose is a combination of four elements;
   i.   A specific **Service** you provide
   ii. To a particular **Group of People**, **Market** or **Person**
   iii. To solve a specific **Problem**
   iv. In return getting some specific **Benefits.**

What you love to do is a clue to where your purpose lies. You will only excel in an activity that you enjoy doing.

You can discover your suitable field of interest by identifying your natural talents since your natural talents or *'Core intelligences'* are coded inside you to give you dominance over your work. An obvious example is singing, for someone who loves to sing and has the right voice for it, singing is an art they can easily dominate and succeed at. It would be pointless to have a wonderful voice but go work at Mc Donald's making burgers.

Other People can recognise your Purpose

Sometimes other people notice your abilities before you do. If people keep saying to you, - you are good in dealing with people. For you working with people is something you can assume success at. If people make regular comments about how well you speak, or how well you analyse things or some other talent or activity you do effortlessly, that should give you a clue on where your strengths lie. It can be;

- The way you sell things and do business, or
- Your passion for change in some field such as politics, education, or
- A concern you have to bring medical healing to sick people, or
- A desire to bring better quality of life to the under privileged, or
- A desire to bring knowledge to an illiterate group of people, or
- A desire to generate finances for some meaningful projects, the list goes on.

YOU WILL ONLY EXCEL IN AN ACTIVITY THAT YOU ENJOY DOING.

I personally am passionate about Leadership and Business. These fields inspire me. They bring me joy, friends and money. I'm always thinking about Systems, Tools, Principles, Techniques and Ideas that can make me effective in these areas. I spend my money on books, magazines, seminars that relate to these subjects. I am in search of ideas, opportunities and relationships that can help me expand in these areas. The books I read and write are in line with these fields. They are my passion and obsession.

Income

Never worry that what you love to do has no potential to make money. That is not true. **You can earn money from anything**. The same way you discovered your purpose in life, you will find ways to use your purpose to attract money. Gordon Ramsey enjoys cooking, so he runs restaurants and a TV program sharing his recipes. Oprah Winfrey, the richest woman in the world enjoys chatting to people and listening to their stories, so she runs a TV program to share the same stories and make fortunes. You can make money from any Talent, Skill or Service.

Many people are pursuing riches instead of purpose; they don't see financial success as connected to their overall purpose in life, which is why so many rich people become unhappy, miserable and self-centred; It is because they have become rich outside of Purpose. **Money is only an energy that allows us to fulfil our dreams, it is only a tool to accomplish purpose. Money is not the end goal but only the means to an end**.

Opportunities

Take note of the **kind of opportunities** that are consistently on your face, they keep coming back to you for a reason. Don't ignore them, they are a clue to where you are supposed to be.

Passion

What you aspire to do, what you secretly want to become or the burning desire inside of you are all indicators that you have the potential to excel at it.

Desire is Potential bursting for Performance. Desire is ability seeking an opportunity to be expressed.

Potential is Excellence before it goes public.

If only you can pin point this work you feel passionate about, you are a step closer to fulfilling your own Great Destiny.

When you do what you love you shine, your natural energy starts to kick in. You feel happier, vivacious, healthier and you even live longer. You don't get easily fatigued, or easily stressed or wearied when you do what you love. You tap into volumes of new energy that you weren't even aware you had. You can rise up early and sleep late and not even notice when you are hungry.

DESIRE IS POTENTIAL BURSTING FOR PERFORMANCE, IT IS ABILITY SEEKING AN OPPORTUNITY TO BE EXPRESSED. POTENTIAL IS EXCELLENCE BEFORE IT GOES PUBLIC.

YOUR ASSIGNMENT IN LIFE IS TO SOLVE A PROBLEM

You can judge if you are on your purpose if someone or a group of people are benefiting from what you do or from the results of your efforts.

In essence, your purpose in life is for the benefit of someone else beside yourself. Your purpose is **not** to machines but to people, even if your work involves spending your day working with machines, computers or animals, but it can only be for the benefit of people. You aught to have people in mind.

Become a Contributor

You were born to serve your Generation.

You were born to be of service to other people not to selfishly spend your life satisfying yourself.

No such purpose is merely to benefit self, that is the very sign that what you are doing is off purpose.

Living a purposeful life is all about serving people.

In the Book of Esther, Esther became the chosen queen of Persia and Media because she was both pretty and smart. She took the position thinking she was in it for a lavish future and a lifestyle of luxury unaware that in the bigger picture of God's plan she was the girl who would risk her life and save the whole Generation of the Jews from being wiped off the face of the earth. It took her uncle Mordecai to wake her up from her selfish thinking, by challenging her;

> "What if you were born for such a time as this." (Esther 4:14).

Let me dare act as your uncle and challenge you;

> "What if you were born for such a time as this?"

What if you were born to be a leader in this generation and help us out in the challenges threatening the endurance of our economy, political stability, social stability, or some other crises facing this generation?

Nelson Mandela the first black President of South Africa found his purpose when he played part in solving a problem which tragically affected his fellow people - *Apartheid*. He believed in a concept, he called – 'Freedom for All'. For anyone to live for such a concept during the government of *Apartheid* in South Africa had to be **tough minded** and willing to pay a high price. *Apartheid* in South Africa was a problem that tragically affected the nation and many people lost their lives to Apartheid. A few courageous individuals including Mr Mandela found their purpose by living to become a solution to that problem.

Just before going to jail for 27 years he was heard saying;

> "Friends, Comrades and all fellow South Africans, I greet you all in the name of Peace, Democracy and Freedom for all. For this is the ideal I hope to live for. But if it need be, it is the ideal I'm prepared to die for".

Driven by love for his country, love for the people and courage to fight, he was willing to pay whatever would be the price for freedom. Twenty seven years later he and other prisoners who were also serving life sentences for demanding ban of Apartheid were given amnesty in their old age. On the day he was released Mr Mandela was asked to give a speech. While people expected an angry prisoner to spit fire balls, Mr Mandela fuelled by love and passion stood up and said;

> "I greet you all in the name of Peace, Democracy and Freedom for all. For this is the ideal I hope to live for but if need be, it is the ideal for which I'm prepared to die".

Purpose driven people are contributors and problem solvers in their generation.

When you become a problem solver, there is a possibility that you will change the world, influence generations and rewrite history.

To be able to pursue a significant mission in life you need a reason greater than just personal gain.

Of the two greatest motivators; fear and love, **love is the greatest force over all**. Love is the strongest reason that motivates people to change, to grow, to give, to sacrifice, to succeed, to win, and to do whatever it takes.

The common thread that ties all the great History Makers is that love was their motivation. Love to entertain people motivated Mohamed Ali to be the best boxer, love for his fellow people motivated Nelson Mandela to serve 27 years in jail so that they can be free, love for human kind motivated Jesus Christ to suffer humiliation and death so that people can be reconciled to God. When your efforts are motivated by love you can pay any price, do whatever it takes, face any challenge, overcome any obstacle to achieve the necessary goal.

Love can endure any amount of pain if it believes that the results are worth the price.

A compelling desire

A compelling desire is another motivator that drives people to do the impossible. When someone has a strong desire to achieve something, even when they are aware that the price involves danger, they will still pay the price, because they are motivated by the final outcome.

No price is too big to beat a strong desire, whatever other force in the world but desire can accomplish just as much.

A strong desire just like a strong reason will command whatever it takes.

- ⊙ Being a Purpose Driven Achiever is not about the work you do, but rather what you mean to the people in your world.

- ⊙ Being a Purpose Driven Achiever is not the powerful position you hold in society but the actions you do that benefit people.
    "The greatest service one can give to God is by serving others" (Napoleon Hill, Author of *Think and grow rich.*)

- ⊙ Being a Purpose Driven Achiever is not being the superstar that everyone worships, but realising your position in your world and occupying it with humility.

⊙ Being a Purpose Driven Achiever does not make you self sufficient and independent but rather integrated to the people you serve and to your generation at large.

⊙ Being a Purpose Driven Achiever is more than being a fully functioning, high performing individual, it is an ability to contribute to your world as a dependable person.

⊙ Being a Purpose Driven Achiever is not about the prestige you get from achieving greatness, it is about what you will become in the process of achieving a worthy cause.

The greatest reward for pursuing your purpose in life is what you become in the challenge of pursuing it.

WHEN YOU BECOME A PROBLEM SOLVER, THERE IS A POSSIBILITY THAT YOU WILL CHANGE THE WORLD, INFLUENCE GENERATIONS AND REWRITE HISTORY.

THERE IS A NEED WAITING FOR YOUR ATTENTION

Gary and Cathy Clark are an Australian couple leading one of the largest Churches in London, - *Hillsong London*. Gary says he believes being on purpose is simply taking a step to meet the needs of people, starting first with those near you. His driving motto is '*Because we can*'. He relates how he and his wife realised a need for a church of the kind in London. He says he doesn't particularly feel he was born to be a pastor, neither did he pray for his purpose to be revealed; but he simply identified a need and that was enough to move him into action. Gary certainly does not imply that it is wrong to pray and ask God for guidance, but speaking for himself he says;

> "I saw the need and thought, if anyone has to do something, it might as well be me."

Being an answer to that need was a start of his purpose journey. He asked God for help, he worked hard and did what he could with the resources he had. Today Gary leads a very prosperous church which supports charity projects in India, Uganda, South Africa and other parts of the world, impacting lives of many disadvantaged children. He says;

> "The problem with most people is that they never take action on the needs around them, they wait endlessly on God to explain what their purpose in life will be, when in fact God is already showing them a need they can do something about."

People who are busy meeting a need that has nothing to do with their selfish interests are happier, fulfilled, excited about life and even popular. As a teenager, I was terribly unhappy; I had no hope, no drive, no real reason to see the future. I struggled with depression and suicidal thoughts. I contemplated and even attempted suicide a few times. I found my breakthrough when I decided what I would live my life for. Suddenly new energy that I had never experienced all my life filled my body and mind. I got a new sense of joy, hope, anticipation and desire to live, to see what I can do during my lifetime. The thief of life prowls around recruiting those who idle, promising them eternal happiness in exchange for their lives. We miss out of the real enjoyment of life when we don't have a meaningful reason to live for. We find no hope for the future until we have a reason to be passionate about, something that drives us to wake up each morning.

Once you have discovered what you will live for, then from that day on; your focus, the direction of your life, your daily activities and the decisions you make are determined by what you have decided to live for. Every activity you do should be relevant to your purpose. **Focus guarantees success.** Your purpose should be the force field radiating itself on to all areas of your life deciding the events you attend, your daily schedule and the people you relate to. Even the resources you get should contribute to the work you have decided to live for.

It is not enough to know your purpose in life, the journey must continue towards a bigger milestone, the goal is to excel. Your aim is to live a life of excellence within your designated purpose. You must shift your focus from mere knowing your purpose in life to the pursuit of excellence.

PART TWO //
THE SEVEN DEADLY PREDATORS OF A PURPOSE CENTERED LIFESTYLE

CHAPTER 08// SEVEN DEADLY PREDATORS OF A PURPOSE CENTERED LIFESTYLE

THE PARABLE OF PREDATORS

Just like weed to a crop, Predators of dreams seek to suffocate and suck life out of dreams. In the biblical parable of the Sower in Mathew Chapter 13; the farmer sowed many seeds, some of his seeds fell on hard ground and got picked up by birds. In this parable birds are predators, and in the light of your dreams predators are spiteful people, dream killers who get fun in killing other people's dreams; people who interfere with your future by speaking failure to your efforts and people who do harmful activities to deter you from achieving your dreams.

Then the parable says some of the farmer's seeds fell on thorny ground; here even though his seeds could germinate to potential maturity but they would be restrained by thorns, and suffer lack of oxygen and die before yielding the expected fruit. In this case the thorns represent the issues of the heart such as;

- ⊙ Unforgiveness
- ⊙ Bitterness
- ⊙ Jealousy
- ⊙ Fear
- ⊙ Doubt

And all their cousins, all have the ability to restrain good dreams, suffer them and kill them before they reach their maturity.

1. FEAR OF LIVING WITHOUT A JOB

A living is not made in a job, you make your living from your life's purpose. Once you know what it is you want to live for, the next step is to figure out how you can make money from it. If you sell it well, to the right customers, there is no reason why you should not make money from it. Historically jobs were not always part of people's lives. People used to live without having to depend on a job. Few centuries back people were self employed in businesses of their interest. No one was interested in working for another except in cases of training and internship. When civilization and labour developments emerged, traders in similar fields started working together in partnerships then jobs were introduced for people who did not have visions of their own. Since then job dependency has grown so popular that people make their living out of working for others.

There are people today whose ultimate dream in life is to just get a nice job. They go to school, work hard through university so that they can just get a nice job that will secure them for life. In the plan of God for humanity, everyone has been given enough potential and creativity to start and build their own dream, but we are too lazy to take the risk of being independent. We are trapped in a dependency mentality.

The Chinese Proverb says;

> "Give a man a fish and you will feed him for a day or teach a man to fish and you feed him for a lifetime."

Prudent people proactively take the step to empower themselves to be good fishers rather than wait for someone else to bring fishes. After all, profits are better than wages.

To pursue a 'dream job' is a dumb idea, just as much as working in a job for the sake of money is wasteful. Pursuing a job keeps you in a holding pattern, keeping you away from doing the things that really matter to you. However you can find a job that helps you learn skills that are necessary to accomplish your life purpose.

A job should be a stepping stone towards your dream. Your primary reason for being in a job should be to learn instead of being in it for money, unless the job brings enough income to finance your dreams or has some other advantages such as allowing you time to do things that really matter to your purpose in life. **If you are going to be in a job anyway, why not find a job that helps you fulfil your dreams instead of neglecting them.**

If you are in the rat race right now, review whether you are in the job that contributes to your dreams or the one that causes you to neglect your dreams. If your dreams are being neglected, then start to work yourself out of that job, before it keeps you in a holding pattern. No job is designed to assist you accomplish your dreams. A company gives you a job solely to generate wealth for the shareholders. What you get as salary is only crumbs, you are hired to be a money making machine for someone who is busy accomplishing their dream. It is up to you to decide what's best for yourself. In a capitalist society the rich get richer in expense of the poor, only the strong minded get a breakthrough.

2. MISAPPROPRIATE APPROACH TO MARRIAGE

In my life time I have come across many myths on purpose but nothing as absurd as the belief that life begins in marriage. Myths can really make comforting excuses when they are sincerely believed. This myth about marriage makes people think if only they get married they have found a reason to live for. Marriage research indicates the contrary; People who marry before they are clear about their life purpose stand a chance to get frustrated in marriage. First you need to be comfortable with your life's purpose then be sure you have sensible reasons for wanting to get married, then get married to someone who is living a purposeful life, otherwise if your reasons are weak you will be tempted to look to your partner to fill the empty feeling inside. That emptiness can only be filled by having a meaningful life even before you get married. **To try and substitute your life's purpose with marriage is forgery**, it will only rob you of your destiny. You will be setting yourself to be the shadow of your partner.

When one of the partners does not know what they are living for, then there is no wholeness in that marriage. First the individuals must be whole then the marriage is whole. Wholeness includes two whole souls meeting together to serve the marriage purpose and still fulfil their individual callings.

Marriage can be a fantastic vehicle to help you fulfil your purpose but it is not a purpose on its own. One of the leading causes of divorce is people who get into marriage with expectations to be rescued from the *purpose vacuum* by the partner. When the partner is unable to fill the emptiness inside they become frustrated and want out. A purposeful approach to marriage is getting into it with intent to serve and support each other, in that way marriage enhances each individual's callings. That way marriage becomes a joy.

Being married to a good partner can be wonderful if they are mature enough to support you in your purpose. It is an error to ignore your purpose because you are married to someone who is actively involved in their purpose and find yourself shadowed behind their strength. You will feel bitter the moment you wake up to realise that you were only just a shadow.

There is yet another extreme; when someone is married but gives more time and effort to their career than their marriage, and so letting the marriage suffer. With time marriage gets strained and finally dies from neglect, because anything neglected long enough will finally die.

Some years ago, a wife of a famous pastor became a famous pastor in her own right running successfully her own powerful ministry. A slight problem emerged in her marriage but she ignored it, never bothered to slow down. She was completely focused and consumed by her ministry. She couldn't get her priorities right and unfortunately for her, few years later the tiny problem had escalated to a massive dilemma which demanded nothing less than her full attention. It was giving her no rest, no sleep, no time to think or focus on her favourite ministry. So she could no longer take the pressure and decided to divorce. She demanded an immediate divorce settlement because she was missing her peace of mind. In spite the efforts from friends to rescue her marriage, she was already too worn out and stressed to listen, she forced the divorce through. But few months later when she had cooled down to realise how her actions had affected her life, she regretted the divorce. She had now lost both her marriage and her favourite ministry. Marriage can be a great vehicle to fulfil purpose, if it is nurtured, respected and given its rightful attention.

In an unhealthy marriage one partner can have their dreams hijacked by the other. A wife of a controlling man can easily find herself in such a position, where she is forced to give up her aspirations to serve the husband's. Don't get this wrong, the Bible states that the wife is her husband's helper, but it does not say she will forsake her own aspirations in exchange for the husband's. It suggests a win-win relationship. It suggests a cooperative team relationship. **Synergy is more fruitful than solo**; if one can chase a thousand then the combined strength of two will take on a ten thousand.

3. OVER COMMITMENT TO YOUR OWN CULTURE

No doubt, we are shaped by both our background and culture. However some cultures are just not structured to promote success. As a result success can be a lonely journey for high achievers who come from limiting cultures. People of the same culture have common traits, common scales of productivity and similar attitudes. People of the same culture have common practices which predetermine the quality of their future. For an example; a culture that is centred around chatting lengthy conversations, excessive relaxation, no hard work, tomorrow is another day, eat-drink-and be happy is unlikely to produce high achievers. The dominant trend in such cultures is poverty and lack. Another culture which is centred on effectiveness, strict respect for time and hard work easily produce leaders, self starters, dreamers, stars and productive individuals. Your culture creates parameters for your success without you being aware. Examine the values of your culture keeping in mind that we are blind to the weaknesses of our own culture.

Over commitment to culture can be a trap to passionate patriots. I usually observe with interest fellow Africans who hold on to backward activities for the sake of keeping customs, refusing to conform to social changes regardless the cost and consequences. They place no value on purpose behind the customs. They are simply committed to maintaining traditions. Needless to say but some of those activities keep people in bondage, poverty, sickness and ignorance. However this is not the case only in Africa, it is like that anywhere, where people are more passionate about their customs than they are about purpose.

4. RELIGIOUS OVERDRIVE

Even though having a relationship with God is supposed to be an enlightening experience but religion proves to be a curse that holds many people from progressing. Religious people get easily trapped in religious rituals, and have no time to work on significant developments. They get caught up in spiritual rituals hoping that God will rescue them from their day to day problems. They give a large percentage of the time to religious activities than acting on solutions to problems. In Joshua chapter 1 when Joshua took over leadership from Moses to lead Israelites to the promised land; Even though prophetically God had already given the promised land to the people of Israel yet Joshua still had to fight real battles to take over what was already given to them. God only gave him a word of blessing;

> "**Be strong and be courageous,** for I have given you the land." (Joshua 1:6)

Now if Joshua was driven by religion, he would have spent few more years asking God to kindly remove the nations occupying the land, but he didn't. He had an understanding of the power of his God, and got out there to fight bloody battles believing that God was with him to help him win. He did not take for granted the blessing of victory given to him, he knew he had to add effort to get victory and so he won every battle and earned the title deed to the Promised Land with sweat and blood.

People who spend too much time praying and not acting produce no results. Any religious activity that is not balanced by equivalent results is wasteful. If you spend ten years praying to get out of poverty and still be in poverty, you are obviously not doing it right. A lesson I got from my grandmother was **prayer and hard work are inseparable**. Her phrase was - *Ora et Labora,* which is Latin for - work and pray. She taught me to pray hard but she also warned me;

> "Never use prayer irresponsibly as an excuse to be lazy, and expect God to do what you should be busy doing yourself."

Gideon in Judges Chapter 6 was a God fearing man and probably very religious too, he sincerely believed that God was going to deliver them Israelites from the exploitation of the Midianites. He got a surprise one day when an angel visited him to tell him;

> "Get up and do something because you are strong enough, you are mighty and able to deliver Israel. What are you really waiting for? Why not use the power that's already in you and stop feeling sorry for yourself, do something then God will give you strength when you need it."

Gideon got up, did what he could, and the people of Israel were delivered in his leadership. Too often religious excitement makes people take a back seat expecting the supernatural to do the natural. In fulfilling your dreams, you will need God's help but be careful that your religious attitude does not make you complaisant.

5. FALSE STARTS

For a long time I could not put my finger on one thing that had stolen most of my early years, but I knew there was a weakness that led to most of my failures until one day I heard someone talk about *false starts*. These are opportunities that appear attractive yet are outside of purpose. Just like on the racing track false starting is starting and not finishing. Sometimes starting good ideas in wrong timing and be forced to drop them prematurely or be forced into a fatal detour. False starters are habitually good starters who never finish anything. They lack accuracy in their steps and timing. They are attracted by '*bling bling*' and glamour in ideas and jump in without counting the cost or considering if they really need to get involved in the idea after all. They end up wasting time, getting depressed, discouraged and drained from immature attempts. False starters end up losing faith in themselves because they have been through too many start-and-drops ultimately end up believing that finishing is impossible.

For many years my life was plagued by false starts until one day I prayed and asked God to order my steps. Proverbs chapter 16 verse 3 says if you commit your plans to the Lord, your efforts will succeed. Since then I waste no time on unfruitful projects. In all your ways acknowledge God, and He will order your steps (Pro 3:6).

6. UNRESOLVED ISSUES OF THE HEART

Unresolved issues of the heart such as unforgiveness and jealousy are self imprisoning. An offended person cannot be productive, they become preoccupied, uncooperative, judgemental and self absorbed because something is blocking their thinking. The only result you can expect from an offended person is bitterness, self destruction, criticism and strife.

There are five groups of people that you must forgive, holding a grudge against any of these will affect your progress and restrain you from thinking clearly. You must;

❶ Forgive Yourself
❷ Forgive God
❸ Forgive your Parents
❹ Forgive your Spouse and
❺ Forgive everyone else you interact with on a daily basis.

The strange thing about unforgiveness is that while you are busy holding grudges against someone; they are out dancing, flourishing and feeling none of your sleepless nights or your grudging pains.

I have learnt from my friend Rocco Van der Merwe who likes talking about issues of the heart that the best way to deal with offences is to develop a preventative attitude, a hard skin towards offences. Since Rocco is aware that offences will always come, he decided long ago to simply forgive his offenders before they do something to offend him, so by the time someone says or does something offensive, they are already forgiven by Rocco. He does this to avoid the pain of carrying offences. So Rocco never wastes his time thinking about what people say or do to offend him. He often quotes his favourite proverb;

> "I have to guard my heart above all else, because it is the source and spring of life." (Proverbs 4:23).

Fear is another heart issue that has potential to obstruct your progress. *FEAR* is simply **F**alse **E**xperiences **A**ppearing **R**eal.

Fear is able to steal dreams and paralyse potential. It demands endless sacrifices and can waste away your time and your destiny. It is always whining;

> "not me"
> "not now"
> "not this one"
> "I can't do it"
> "I don't have the right background"
> "I don't have what it takes"

All such thinking and words only make you more aware of your fears instead of helping you overcome. If you scare yourself by expecting failure, you will get nothing but failure. In fact, it is proven that whatever a person fears will be attracted. Job 3:25 says;

"For what I fear comes upon me, and what I dread befalls me".

A man who had a terrible fear of electric shock was seated on an electric chair to help him overcome his fear. He was so fearful; he believed that if he sat on an electric chair he would die, so he sat and tragically he died; meanwhile the chair was not even connected to the electricity. **Really, if there is anything to fear, it is fear itself.**

Though not all fear is bad, positive fear will make you run away from danger. It will make you work harder to save your job, or keep traffic rules to avoid getting fined, or save lots of money to avoid poverty. But negative fear will paralyze your hopes, victimize you, steal your dreams and leave you in suffering. Fear is not only the obstacle to achieving your destiny, it is also damaging to your health and to your self confidence. It denies you of the happiness you really deserve. Fear does not have to be final, as the American author Susan Jeffers says it; "Feel the fear and do it anyway."

Courage is not the absence of fear, but the brave choice to do it anyway. Make a vow to face your fears and overcome them. Be determined to fear nothing. Remember fear is learnt, no one is born fearful, and therefore fear can be unlearned by learning to be courageous instead. The more you take risks, the more your fears dwindle down and the stronger your courage rises.

I developed a personal strategy to deal with fear; whenever fear attacks me I fight it back with words of faith and courage. When a thought of fear comes, I overwhelm it with words of victory until it disappears. I rhyme words like;

"God has not me a spirit of fear, but a spirit of power."

"I am bold and fearless."

"I am a more than a conqueror."

"I am destined to win not fail."

"Victory is my portion not defeat."

"I will overcome every obstacle and every challenge."

I repeat these words to myself until I feel genuine boldness and courage rise within me overriding every kind of fear.

COURAGE IS NOT THE ABSENCE OF FEAR, BUT THE BRAVE CHOICE TO DO IT ANYWAY.

---

7. HOW YOU SEE YOUR AGE

Elvira was 71 when I met her in Magaliesburg, South Africa, born and bred in Arizona, had never been to Africa before. She was slightly hard of hearing but strong and ready for an intensive training to work with wild South African youth. Our motto at Youth For Christ was RFA – Ready For Anything, this was hardly possible for me age 21 due to many obstacles we faced such as carrying heavy Audio Visual equipment, sleepless nights, early mornings and long days. But Elvira was ready for it all, never prepared to back off or mention her age as an excuse for lack of performance. She was blessed with energy of a horse. During that year she spent working with the Youth For Christ Team, she saw thousands of young lives being changed. She helped organise programs and solved many teenage issues and was determined live young and have fun. Everybody called her a blessing. Her age slowed her down at times but the 71 year old Elvira was forever willing and determined to live life to the full.

Do you think you are just too old or too young to pursue your purpose? It may be true in some cases that younger people are more unclear about their future than older, but there are exceptions. David's purpose started manifesting at a young age as a warrior for Israel. During his visit to see his brothers at war he found an opportunity to act in his purpose by leading the battle killing the war stopper Goliath. At a tender age he led a series of battles and won everyone of them, to the extent that a national song was composed about his victories 'Saul has killed his thousands but David has killed ten thousand more'. He knew his purpose was to be a worrier for Israel and he was ready to fight battles and win. He did not once think – oh, I'm just a kid, if these big adults can't fight this giant there's just no chance for me. He was head strong and confident of what he could do and what his God was able to do through him. You can never be too young to do what you were born to do. Regardless your age, you can at least start to prepare yourself because soon when the opportunity comes, it should find you ready.

Recently I took Alex and Damien out to Pizza Hut, both age 18. For the first few minutes of our conversation while enjoying the first slices of pizza we talked a lot about nothing. Until I dropped the question;

> "So you boys are finishing A-levels soon, then what? University I guess. But what exactly do you want to do with your lives?"

It was a long silence for the first time at our table, both boys chewing endlessly starring at me baffled, waiting on each other to say something. Alex finally broke the silence and said;

> "Well, I'm going to invest at the stock market."
> "Have you started making a research about the stock market?" I challenged him.

He looked at me even longer chewing deliberately slow with a blushing smile as if I caught him off guard. He swallowed slowly, then reminded me;

"I am only 18 you know."

I responded;

"I know that, and I guess it is the best age to start getting involved in the stock markets now, right?"

Damian rescued him;

"We are going to be millionaires by age 30, but it's still a bit early to get excited about that now."

"OK" I responded.

"I guess if you start working on it now it can only increase your chances to be millionaires by age 30. Why not start reading books on investing in the stock market, read about different types of shares and options and start saving money towards building your own portfolios, you have only 12 years to thirty. Otherwise before you know it, you will be interrupted by other interesting things in life, that will block your desire to be millionaires."

Here my young English friends politely pushed the topic out to talk about Arsenal's last game, as if our topic was spoiling the moment. The point here is that you can never be too young to think about your future. The sooner you start the better for you.

Many adults wish they had started earlier in life but just that they did not have the opportunities or the motivation, or someone to guide them. Now is the best time to pursue your purpose.

Parents instead of demanding your children to make up for your past failures, you should be motivating them to think about their own future and to start making decisions early in life. Children are entitled to their own purpose in life. They should not be forced to forfeit their dreams to pursue parents' unfulfilled dreams, they should be motivated to take control of their own dreams.

THE FINAL WORD

When Helen Keller was 19 months old she contracted an illness that left her deaf, dumb and blind. She learnt to read and write in Braille. Helen became the first deaf and blind person to get a Bachelor of Arts degree at Redcliff College Cambridge, Massachusetts. She became a brilliant author and an activist, fighting against the injustices of war. She founded the Helen Keller home for children and travelled the world lecturing. Helen knew no limits. When she was asked;

> "Can you think of anything worse than being blind and deaf?"

Helen said;

> "Yes, it is to be able to see and have no Vision."

So, what could be your excuse?

Whatever your reason is, that wants to keep you from fulfilling your purpose is a thief. It wants to take the most important thing - your right to live a fulfilled and significant life.

There is an inner witness inside you that confirms whether you are on purpose or not. If you are experiencing joy in what you do, you must be in your purpose. If not, then its time to make a change.

If you are not excited about life or have lost your sense of expectation and hope, that is a sign you are off purpose.

If your life is chaotic, enduring poverty, or lacking friends; those are external signs indicating that you may be busy outside of your purpose. These are common conditions indicating that it is time to make a change, it is time to re-evaluate your priorities and seek new possibilities.

If your life delivers conditions you don't want, don't just settle hoping things will get better, declare a state of emergency and begin a fight against every force that is holding you back. Never allow your life to be wasted away by excuses. Get up and do something.

A life that is defended by excuses has become comfortable in defeat, it has settled for mediocrity and is destined for failure.

Whatever you tolerate you will never change.

Whatever you think is your limitation, however valid you think it is, it is a thief aiming to steal and kill your unborn dreams. You can stop the thief before it wastes your potential.

> *A LIFE THAT IS DEFENDED BY EXCUSES HAS BECOME COMFORTABLE IN DEFEAT, IT HAS SETTLED FOR MEDIOCRITY AND IS DESTINED FOR FAILURE.*

From now on, find motivations not excuses. **An excuse gives you a reason why you should accept mediocrity, but a motivation gives you a reason why you should pursue excellence.**

PRACTICAL TIPS

SELF ESTEEM AND CONFIDENCE

❖ DRESS UP IN ATTIRE THAT MAKES YOU FEEL COMFORTABLE, GREAT AND ATTRACTIVE. LOVE YOURSELF AND BELIEVE IN YOURSELF!

❖ GET UP IN THE MORNING, LOOK AT THE MIRROR, SPEAK POSITIVELY TO YOURSELF, LOUD AND PASSIONATELY - "GOOD MORNING GORGEOUS! YOU ARE GOING TO HAVE A GREAT DAY."

❖ AFFIRM YOURSELF WITH WORDS THAT CONFIRM WHO YOU WANT TO BE. MAKE YOUR STATEMENTS IN PRESENT TENSE. DO THIS SEVERAL TIMES IN A DAY WITH A STRONG FIRM CONVINCED TONE OF VOICE; "I AM DESTINED FOR GREATNESS, I WAS ENGINEERED SUCCESS, I WAS BORN FOR A SIGNIFICANT PURPOSE"

❖ MAKE A LIST OF ALL THE THINGS THAT HAPPENED IN YOUR PAST THAT NEGATIVELY AFFECTED YOUR SELF ESTEEM, MAKE A CEREMONY WHERE YOU BURN THE LIST AND VERBALLY DECLARE THAT NON OF THOSE THINGS WILL AFFECT YOU EVER AGAIN; "I NOW PUT TO PAST ALL THAT HAS TO DO WITH MUM AND DAD'S DIVORCE. I AM FREE OF ANYTHING THAT HAS TO DO WITH THEIR DIVORCE AND I FORGIVE BOTH OF THEM FOR EVERY WRONG THEY CAUSED ME. I AM FREE!"

PURPOSE

❖ *To decide on a suitable purpose to pursue. First pray about it, then make a list of all things that attract your attention. Then make another list prioritising them according to what you really love and enjoy doing. Take special notice of the top three. For example;.*

    ❶ *To work with animals*
    ❷ *To be an astronaut*
    ❸ *To work with kids*

❖ *Write a statement that presents your purpose, print it and hang it visibly on the wall.*

❖ *Collect items such as wall pictures, music, articles, stories, books, magazines that relate to your purpose and surround yourself with it. Example; Pictures of experts who dominate your field of purpose.*

❖ *Start to learn more about how you can become significant in your purpose.*

❖ *Use Self-affirmations, strong positive words, self suggestions and scriptures to affirm the future you want. Do this daily.*

❖ *Maximise use of your sub conscious mind; Influence it with scripture, words of motivation and words of hope. Review your goals daily memorise them. Repeat this for 30 days until your subconscious recites them without your conscious involvement and plays pictures of your dreams even when you are busy with your daily activities.*

❖ *USE CREATIVE VISUALISATION TO YOUR ADVANTAGE- USE PROPS WHICH PAINT THE PICTURE OF YOUR DREAMS SUCH AS PHOTOS AND POSTERS, EVEN SET TIME ASIDE FOR CREATIVE THINKING.*

❖ *ADOPT A POSITIVE MENTAL ATTITUDE (PMA) –RELAX AND CLEAR YOUR MIND FROM THOUGHTS OF FRUSTRATION, BITTERNESS, AND ANGUISH. ONLY ALLOW CALM AND CREATIVE THOUGHTS. RELAX YOUR MIND, BE COOL. RELAX YOUR FACIAL EXPRESSIONS. LEARN THE SKILL OF ALLOWING ONLY THE THOUGHTS YOU WANT AND BLOCKING ALL UNWANTED THOUGHTS UNTIL THEY ARE COMPLETELY DISMISSED.*

EPILOGUE

The end of anything is the beginning of something new. As this book comes to its end, I trust it means a new beginning for you. My hope is that your life be never the same again. You have much to give and much to live for. From the one whom much is given, much will be expected. I pray that you will never run out of hope, passion, and drive to be the best you can be. I trust that you will close this book inspired, encouraged, and equipped to excel and flourish. And I hope you will witness in your own life changes as a result of our walk together through the pages of this book.

Please write me, I would love to hear from you. Tell me your personal story, how you are getting on in your Journey of Excellence. Also invite me, I would be honoured to visit your group and share more on these issues. My last secret for you before I disappear is - read this book again, you will be surprised how much you discover by rereading a book. God bless you. Live with passion and dare to live without limits!

ACKNOWLEDGEMENTS

A special thanks to all my friends, especially;

To my mother Nomsa, for her motivation and prayers.

To Norma Hessel for always sending a word of encouragement during my tough season.

To everyone at Downtown, East London, SA; especially the pastors; Maureen, Rocco, Les and Mr Bikitsha.

At Basingstoke; to Helen the Scott, Isaac and the Tala family, Jolanta and Lukasz Zajac, Corine Goddard and her family for giving me second home away from home.

To Tim Salmon for seeing potential in me and for his motivation.

To my cousins Unathi, Thulani, uncle Thozi, my brother Jeph, my friends Gibson, Bheki, & Sizwe.

I appreciate all your support; **I am convinced there is no such a thing as DIY** (Do-It-Yourself) **success.**

BOOK SUMMARY

This book is for Uncommon People. It will stir you up and inspire you to think differently from the crowd. It will sharpen your uncommonness and bring out the Achiever in you. It will challenge you to grow in Purpose and in Excellence. It will boost your confidence and productivity in your Career and your Field of Calling. Every page in this book is packed with passion. You will be motivated to break your limits and become an Uncommon Purpose Driven Achiever. This book is Powerful, Charming, written with Style, Grace and Humour.

www.TheJourneyofExcellence.com

ABOUT THE AUTHOR

Oscar Bonga Nomvete (MBA MSc) is a Leadership and Management Consultant. He facilitates Leadership workshops and seminars for Non-Governmental Organizations, Churches and Corporate Companies. His Passion is to train people on the Principles that enhance Personal, Management and Leadership Effectiveness. He inspires people to become Leaders in their Careers and Fields of calling.

He started his career as a Youth Worker, working for Charity Organisations such as *Youth For Christ* where he worked in numerous countries in Africa and in the USA. He is the Managing Director of First Pinnacle LTD, a London based Consulting Firm, an Entrepreneur, a Public Speaker and a Teacher.

BOOKS BY THE AUTHOR

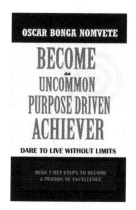

www.TheJourneyofExcellence.com
oscar.bonga@yahoo.co.uk